Myrzabek Tuiganov

Issues of Islam's transformation in Kazakhstan

Myrzabek Tuiganov

Issues of Islam's transformation in Kazakhstan

ScienciaScripts

Cover image: www.ingimage.com

This book is a translation from the original published under ISBN 978-3-330-33193-8.

Publisher:
Sciencia Scripts
is a trademark of
Dodo Books Indian Ocean Ltd. and OmniScriptum S.R.L publishing group

120 High Road, East Finchley, London, N2 9ED, United Kingdom
Str. Armeneasca 28/1, office 1, Chisinau MD-2012, Republic of Moldova, Europe
Printed at: see last page
ISBN: 978-620-8-28287-5

Table of Contents

Tuiganov M.S.

The collection includes scientific articles by the author devoted to the issues of transformation of Islam in modern Kazakhstan. It shows relevant aspects of the politicization of Islam, its relationship with the state, as well as the problems of radicalization.

The publication may be useful for undergraduates, masters, doctoral students and for those who practically deal with religious issues.

RADICALIZATION OF ISLAM IN KAZAKHSTAN: AN INSTITUTIONAL APPROACH

Abstract: The article deals with issues related to the radicalization of Islam in Kazakhstan. The study of some aspects of the process of radicalization of Islam is proposed through the analysis of current events and application of institutional approach. The peculiarities of correlation of traditional Islam and radical current of Islam as social institutions within the political system of Kazakhstan are shown.

Keywords: radicalization, Islam, institution, institutionalization, institutional approach, traditional Islam, political system

Religion is increasingly involved in all spheres of life in Kazakhstani society. This is an objective process of post-secular development, one of the important features of which has been the respectability of religion in general, and Islam in particular. Therefore, the institutionalization of radicalism in Kazakhstan can take place unnoticed against the background of general Islamic revival and low religious consciousness of the society. Recognition of the fact of radicalization of Islam and the struggle against it creates a special atmosphere with inherent ideal images of "victory", and at the same time existential fears.

Ideologically, society must see an image of "victory" over radicalism. The mission of the state should be to develop this "desired image of victory. This image must be drawn from the institutional environment itself. The problem is that the radicals have already proposed their own image of "victory," quite simple and clear, consisting, first of all, in the establishment of the so-called World Caliphate - an ideal version of society and state for all mankind.

Retrospective analysis shows that the realization of the idea of the World Caliphate is based not only on the tenets of radical ideology, but the principle of the global concept of sustainable development, expressed in the motto: "Think globally, act locally", is inadvertently extrapolated to it. The principle is universal, and the actions of radical institutions according to this principle allow creating a cumulative effect on society and politics.

Historically, religion as a social institution has been a kind of regulator of political activity, influencing political systems and the subsequent transformation of religiously oriented social space. The state, in turn, used religion to achieve geopolitical goals. Such interaction was two-way and mutually conditioned, so it is not accidental that these two institutions both in the past and in the present continue to have a profound impact on the civilizational development of the world and on man himself [1, p. 214]. At the present stage, the situation around religion in Kazakhstan can be formulated as a dichotomy - "promoting the positive construction of confessionally stable, spatial and temporal forms of being of society" against "mechanisms that cause changes and transformations of ethno-confessional space". One of these mechanisms was the processes of politicization and radicalization of Islam, associated with the sacralization of state power and religious expansion. According to A. L. Strizoe's concept of politicization of communities ".... religious communities" have "autonomy of functioning and development", and the level of politicization of ethno-religious communities depends on the conditions of socio-political stability [Cited in 1, p. 214].

In the words of A. Raymond, one of the classics of political science: "All human interaction presupposes the presence of power. In every religion, power is clearly expressed. Its uniqueness lies in the fact that a religious person is subject to two authorities - the authority of God and the authority of man (his leader). In radical organizations, the leader usurps all these authorities in his hands. As for politics, it can become religious, and religiosity does not necessarily have to be expressed in the traditional understanding of religion. As we know, totalitarian ideology is a vivid example of secular religion.

To begin with, let us disclose the content of key terms. Radicalism *(from Late Latin radicalis - radical, Latin radix - root)* is socio-political ideas and actions aimed at decisive change of existing institutions. Radicalization is understood as an accelerated, more decisive development of any process, phenomenon, etc. [2]. This term in the scientific literature on the problems of Islamism is often used as a synonym along with such terms as politicization of Islam, extremism, terrorism. Radicalism implies dissociation from the existing tradition. In history, it has also been applied to moderate reformist movements. Religious radicalism relies on dogma, which forms a cognitive assessment of social reality, followed by a new variation of reforming this reality.

In this article, we understand radicalization of Islam as "a political process based on the ideological doctrine of radical Islam (Islamism), which involves the implementation of differentiated specific political practices - from the implementation of the so-called "Islamic call" (moderate radicalism) to the total conduct of subversive and terrorist actions against the "enemies of Islam", justifying it by the "struggle for faith" - jihad - in order to build a "struggle for faith" (jihad). (moderate radicalism) to total subversive and terrorist actions against the "enemies of Islam", justifying it by the "struggle for faith" - jihad, in order to build an Islamic state and the introduction of Sharia law (ultra-radicalism)" [3]. [3].

If we talk about institutionalism, we should first of all note that it is one of the modern methodological concepts gaining popularity in the scientific community. G. Bloomer found the essence of social institutions in active subjects and action: "Human society should be seen as consisting of active people, and the life of society should be seen as consisting of their actions. There is also collective action that causes individuals to adapt their lines of behavior to each other. At the specific societal level, D.G. Mead considers a number of statements about social institutions, defining them "as the social response of society," as "the vital customs of society," as "an organized set of attitudes." They do not restrain creativity, determine how people should act, leaving space for individual and creativity [Cited in 4, p. 125]. One way or another, G. Bloomer and D.G. Mead mean by institutions the activity substances. Communications play an important role in them, but the description omits structural elements that ensure the stability of institutions.

In the framework of the problem under consideration, we consider religious *activity in* general, and the *process of* radicalization of Islam, in particular, as a socio-political institution, as a united, to a certain extent, expedient, from the point of view of the actors themselves, action. It should be noted that the basis of this expediency is the political space, which is not only a form of human interaction, but also a system of coordinates for the development of society.

Islam in Kazakhstan is not an innovative social institution, as its spread in the region has a thousand-year history, but despite this at the present stage it has acquired a number of specific characteristics. This is due to the general logic of the emergence and development of social institutions in the conditions of independent Kazakhstan.

From the perspective of institutionalism, the process of radicalization of Islam in Kazakhstan can be considered in the following aspects. First, the replenishment of the ranks of neophytes of religious extremist organizations and the establishment of their active activities in the field of "confessional conversion" at the expense of the formation of a marginal core in Kazakh society. Extensive marginal core, especially in the youth environment, as a rule, became, on the one hand, a consequence of the existing historical situation, some errors of the internal policy of the state, and on the other hand, extensive work of specific actors-radicals and globalization. All these phenomena can be presented as internal and external institutional resources aimed at strengthening and more or less clear-cut formalization of the institutional positions of radical Islam as an intra-country (individual, Kazakhstani), and as an integral part of the global one. The fact that Kazakhstan is an important strategic object of activity of extremists of the world level is confirmed, for example, by the fact that "one of the most important field commanders of Bin Laden, Abu Leit al-Libi, was "a kind of "Authorized Representative of Al Qaeda's leadership in Central Asia" before his death in 2008" [5, p. 73]. [5, c. 73]. Undoubtedly, the missionary activities of radicals and their results show what stable positions they have taken in regulating the religious sphere of a certain part of Kazakh society. Despite all the efforts of the state and the public, their quantitative and qualitative reduction is extremely slow. For example, in the analytical report based on the results of the sociological study "Evolution of an Islamist in Kazakhstan - from an ordinary believer to a terrorist", conducted by the staff of the Center for Security Programs and the Public Foundation "Center for Social and Political Research "Strategy" in 2013, the majority of those convicted of extremist and terrorist crimes, despite the fact that they have abandoned radical views, still do not abandon an unconventional understanding of Islam. "According to the results of the interviews, among those convicted to this day remain committed to the ideas of Salafism, which glorifies life according to Sharia and does not recognize traditional Islam. It is clear that in this case the ideas of fundamental Islam have turned into a life attitude, and the Islamic state is an ideal state in which "they" (*author*) want to live"" [6, C. 11]. An undesirable scenario of institutionalization of radical Islam, where the essence of social institutions can be found in the acting subjects and actions, and the presence and expansion, even at the level of regions (mainly in the south and west of the Republic of Kazakhstan), of the community of radicalized citizens, over time can lead to the formation of collective action, which will force individuals to adapt their lines of behavior to new conditions. In essence, we may end up with an uncontrolled institutional environment.

Secondly, the goals of terrorist acts are not limited to mass intimidation and self-promotion, as many people claim. The terrorist acts committed on the territory of the republic give institutional content not only to the actually existing radical Islam (as a socio-political institution), but also to its ideal image embodied in the popular perception and, of course, in the notorious political mythology. In the resulting static image, only the consequence remains - a relatively unified and rationally acting organism striving to achieve its self-established goals. The inter-institutional social relations that created the very space in which the "radical core" is able to operate and from which it derives its goals - the institutional environment - are overlooked.

Thirdly, radicalization of Islam refers to hidden processes. As we know, there are explicit and hidden processes in the political sphere. The formation and activities of radicals are set in motion by institutions or social groups that do not have proper legal formalization, by interactions between constituent parts of civil society on a small scale. Therefore, even new legislation in the sphere of state-confessional relations cannot solve the whole problem. The authorities face a difficult dilemma: on the one hand, tougher legislation may lead to increased radicalization and conspiracy of Islamists, while on the other hand, weakening of control will not go unnoticed by radicals and will be used by them for their own purposes.

As for traditional Islam, the new historical situation played a dual role. On the one hand, the processes of democratization and the corresponding normative-legal base gave Islam the opportunity to form its new "construction", which had to fit into the general course of socio-political, socio-economic and spiritual development of society, provided an opportunity to build its own, perhaps the broadest for the entire history of Kazakhstan, version of relations according to the formula "religion - society - state". On the other hand, it is traditional Islam that has become the object of reproaches from the general public for condoning the radicalization of Islam. These reproaches range from the "silent indifference" of traditionalists to accusations of some "indirect assistance" to the radicalization of religion. The latter is based on the facts of uncontrolled delegation of candidates to study in foreign Islamic educational institutions, as well as the sermons of extremists (e.g. Said Buryatsky) in mosques.

Of course, we do not agree with such a statement of the question. Looking for the culprit is the easiest thing to do, and sticking to such a position, we risk repeating the mistake of "soviet" fatalism, and it is difficult and scary to predict what will happen to traditional faith in such a scenario. In addition, the search for culprits is an indicator of dogmatization of state political power. At the present stage, in the conditions of formation and strengthening of democratic institutions represented by public associations and religious organizations, it will be natural and appropriate to apply new political technologies to debunk radical cells and their activities with the involvement of the general public. Attempts and some results in this area are already available.

An important issue is the institutional relationship between radical Islam and tardic Islam. From the point of view of religious theory, traditional Islam ignores the conclusions of radicals, and thus considers them dilettantes in the field of theology, who rely on the facts and dogmas they need to build their ideology. In Kazakhstan, the DUMK is fighting radicalism in this direction. In addition, the DUMK, together with the offices of the Ministry of Religious Affairs, holds events dedicated to explaining the concepts of secularism to the general public. Thus, the state, having given such a preference to the official leadership of the Muslims of Kazakhstan, exposes the DUMK as a "mouthpiece" of state-confessional relations in the republic. Such institutionalization of traditional Islam in the space of politics contributes to increasing the authority of the DUMK not just as a religious organization, but as a socio-political institution, strengthens the gap between radical and traditional Islam, and certainly shifts the DUMK to the center of the political system.

Thus, the application of institutional approach shows some essential aspects of radicalization of Islam in Kazakhstan, reveals the features of political technologies in the sphere of state-confessional relations. Radicalization of Islam is a multidimensional phenomenon, and a more effective application of institutional methodology in its study requires its further development.

Literature

1. Drinova E.M. Confessional geopolitics and processes

Politicization of religion // Bulletin of Volgograd State University. Series 7: Philosophy. Sociology and Social Technologies. №2, 2008. - С. 214-218;

2. Philosophical Encyclopedic Dictionary. - Moscow: Soviet Encyclopedia. Editor-in-chief: L.F. Ilyichev, P.N. Fedoseev, S.M. Kovalyov, V.G. Panov. 1983. [Electronic resource]. - URL: http://dic.academic.ru/dic.nsf/es/137391/радикализм. (Date of circulation 27.01.2015);
3. Hajibekov R.G. Internal factors of influence on the processes of politicization and radicalization of Islam in the Russian Federation: dissertation ... Candidate of political sciences: 23.00.02 / Hajibekov Ruslan Gadzhibekovich; [Place of defense: Russian Academy of National Economy and Public Administration under the President of the Russian Federation]. - Rostov-on-Don, 2013.- 177 p.: ill. RGB OD, 6114-23/62 . [Electronic resource]. - URL: http://www.dslib.net/polit-instituty/vnutrennie-faktory-vlijanija-na-processesy-politizacii-i-i-radikalizacii-islama-v.html (Date of address 28.01.2015 г.);
4. Luke G.A. Social innovation design in regional youth policy. Samara: Izd-vo "Samara University", 2003. - 278 с.;
5. Karin E. "Soldiers of the Caliphate": Myths and Reality. Almaty 2014. - 173 с.;
6. "Evolution of an Islamist in Kazakhstan - from an ordinary believer to a terrorist" (Analytical report on the results of the sociological research). Center for Security Programs and Public Foundation "Center for Social and Political Research "Strategy", - Almaty 2013, 13 p.

On the Politicization of Islam in Kazakhstan: Essence and Trends

Abstract: The main ways of the process of politicization of Islam in Kazakhstan, essential characteristics and main tendencies are considered. The concept of politicization of Islam and its classification in the context of the development of state-confessional relations in the Republic of Kazakhstan are presented.

Key concepts: religion, politicization, Islam, radicalism.

Contemporary political struggles revolve around two interrelated issues: resources and decision-making centers. Expropriation of resources or exclusion from participation in decisions are the two main indicators of social disadvantage. And since "resource" in post-industrial society has become not only traditional means, but also education, science, health care, culture, leisure, politics has lost its direct correlation with the so-called "production relations"; interest group and pressure group (i.e. those who claim a share of resources and those who claim to participate in decisions) arise in all spheres [11, p. 283]. The emergence of these groups is directly related to the process of politicization of social relations.

Politicization explodes everyday life, makes obvious the failure of habitual approaches to solving existing problems, legitimizes the ignoring of previously established and obsolete rules and norms. It not only assumes, but also justifies the use of extraordinary means and methods of doing business [4, p. 80].

That is, politicization implies the movement of the political field or political meanings to other spheres of social reality, actualized at a certain historical stage. In modern conditions, virtually all spheres of social life are subjected to politicization. One of the main reasons is the compensation of the power factor in modern politics by softer social technologies - economic, spiritual, informational. In addition to the above, politicization is also a technology of social relations management.

The famous thinker of the New Age Sh. Montesquieu considered the role of religion as one of the effective factors of influence on the organization of social life [3, p. 53]. To identify the essence of politicization of religion, the sociocentric approach is complemented by the anthropocentric one.

Modern anthropological research has confirmed the old truth: man is a metaphysical and religious being, seeking meaning [12, p. 53]. According to O. Comte, religion allows a triple division inherent in the nature of man. It includes an intellectual aspect, dogma; an affective aspect, love, which is expressed in a cult; and a practical aspect, which Comte calls "mode". The cult orders the feelings; the mode orders the personal or social behavior of the believers. Religion reproduces in itself the differentiation of human nature: generating unity, it must appeal simultaneously to reason, feeling, and action, i.e., to all human faculties [14, p. 116.]. Religious consciousness is included in the vast sphere of the imaginary (ideas, beliefs, perceptions, symbols, images), and it is impossible to expel from this sphere the religious, acting in it as an equal to other "specific" dimensions, including the political [17, p. 256].

In this regard, the definition given in the Westminster dictionary is interesting, where politicization is understood as giving political character to actions or lines of behavior [5].

The politicization of religion as a social institution and a subject of social relations is predetermined by the universality of political power. According to A. Strizoe, in its field (political power) can be any social subject and any problem (from personal reputation and technical characteristics of the product, to religious, artistic or scientific disputes) [15, c. 280].

Some authors note that the very separation of religious entities from political institutions already contains the root of independent political considerations [1, p. 4-5].

Politics influences religion by regulating public life, creating legal boundaries for its vital activity, forming a climate of mutual respect and tolerance between confessional communities, protecting the rights of citizens to freedom of conscience, as well as regulating the legal status of religious organizations. In turn, the political process develops and is conditioned not only by the boundaries of the existing relations of political forces and the nature of the political system, but also by the spiritual ideals and principles formed in society. The latter, by the way, are determined in society by religious teachings [11, p. 45]. Consequently, religion, being a purely subjective element of human existence, can affect not only the values, beliefs and emotions of people, but also determine their behavior in the sphere of political relations.

In addition, according to political science, religion fulfills 4 main functions in the political sphere: 1. Legitimate function, is performed by religion when the religious position supports or, on the contrary, besieges the power, its ideas or actions. 2. Representative function, consists in the expression and protection of the interests of some group of people by religious organizations that act as subjects of politics. 3. Differentiating function, stipulates the existence of boundaries of division of spheres of influence of different religions. 4. Integrating function, manifested in the realization of the huge integrating potential of religion [1, p. 5].

Thus, religion and politics are in close interrelation, serving each other and fulfilling complementary roles depending on the situation. In the case of modern Kazakhstan, it should be remembered that a country where religion has been "outlawed" for many years, even Islam, as the religion of the indigenous ethnos, cannot be a subject of "dialog of equals". The state has an advantage, even despite the dynamics of the population's religiosity. For example, according to the results of a social survey among young people in 2016 to the question "Do you consider yourself a believer?" 71% of respondents answered positively, among them 73.5% were Kazakhs. To the question "What led you to faith?" 57.9% answered: "Upbringing in the family". Thus, 14% of the surveyed youth came to religion consciously, independently and their religious socialization took place regardless of family upbringing

Of course, it would be wrong of us to speak about the religiosity of citizens only on the basis of one question, but, nevertheless, the high percentage of positive answers already shows the attitude and sympathy of the society, in particular of young people, to religion in general.

Politicization of the activities of confessions and religious groups, emphasizes in his abstract D.G. Mirzakhanov, is expressed in the desire of some religious figures to extend their influence in the sphere of political relations, culture and education, in the demand for revision and in direct disregard of the provisions of the legislation of the Russian Federation on the separation of religious associations from the state. The extreme and most dangerous form of politicization of religion and expressed clericalism is the manifestation of religious and political extremism [10, p.5].

E.M. Drinova notes: "The mechanisms causing changes and processes transformations of ethno-confessional space should be subjected to a comprehensive analysis. One of such mechanisms was the processes of politicization of religion, associated with the sacralization of state power, religious expansion, ethno-confessional conflicts of confessional partogenesis" [5, p. 214-215] [5, c. 214-215].

In the light of the problem we have outlined, the presented positions can be applied to many spatial and temporal facts of interaction between the state and religion, conditionally dividing them into three categories: 1. The desire of some religious figures to extend their influence on the sphere of political relations, culture and education, sacralization of state power; 2. The demand for revision and direct ignoring of the provisions of legislation in the sphere of religion; 3. Manifestation of religious-political extremism, the consequence of which can be ethno-confessional conflicts and religious expansion. At the same time, each subsequent option is socially more "dangerous".

Based on the above, we believe that in the current conditions of Islam's renewal, it is advisable to differentiate the process of its politicization by the degree of influence of Islamic and Islamist ideas, the activities of relevant organizations and Muslim religious figures on the political system.

It should be noted that the processes taking place in the sphere of Islam are called differently by scholars - "revival of Islam", "return of Islam", "Islamic renewal", "re-Islamization" and others. We agree with the opinion of D. Wilkowski's opinion in the designation of these processes as "Islamic renewal" or "re-Islamization", where "renewal" means not only the legitimization of official Islam and its administrative registration in the form of the Spiritual Administration of Muslims of Kazakhstan, but also the emergence of religious organizations, such as youth and women's associations, which did not exist before, as well as the development of the system of religious education. The phenomenon of Islamic renewal also includes the presence of so-called exogenous factors in the Islamic life of the country, more precisely the presence of foreign, primarily Arab Islamic foundations and organizations that finance and materially support emerging Islamic movements [2, p. 22-23].

Using Russia as an example, E.M. Drinova identifies the following models of Islam's politicization:

"The development of the secular model of Islam. This model is characterized by the declarative nature of Islamic revival, a high level of tolerance between Muslims and Orthodox. At the same time, the emergence of new, as a rule, external value orientations led to a significant rapprochement between nationalists and religious Muslim figures. As a result, radical Islamic political organizations appeared in the republic in the 1990s, which, according to R. Mukhametshin, in the distant future may lead to the formation of another model of Islamic fundamentalism;

- formation of a model of Islamic radicalism (Dagestan, Karachay-Cherkessia, Kabardino-Balkaria). The processes of radicalization of Islam were associated with the emergence of a large number of educational and missionary organizations of the Near and Middle East. The political ambition of the leaders of ultra-radical movements, irreconcilable ideology, inability to adequately assess the situation and lack of political experience - all this led to the fact that the Islamic movement seriously discredited itself in the eyes of the population.

The idea of symbiotic unity of Russian "Orthodox nationalism" and Islamic parties was put into the formation of the next model, which never reached its logical conclusion.

Similar tendencies of Islam's denationalization are most fully traced in the Central Asian post-Soviet republics" - summarizes the author [5, p. 217-218].

Based on the proposed typology and applying the structural-functional approach, we justified the following models of politicization of Islam in Kazakhstan:

- A secular model that includes two sub-models:

1. *Symbiosis.* Political behavior is often determined by religious values, foreign and domestic policy of states is built in accordance with religious interests. However, on the other hand, the use of the mechanism of manipulating public opinion with the help of religious concepts is becoming more and more popular, religion is exploited in the interests of ruling elites, in particular, in the field of increasing their own legitimacy [11, p. 45].

This process can be characterized as follows. Religion, not claiming, at least openly, to participate in political interactions, becomes involved in them at the "suggestion", the initiative of political elites. The tone of this "suggestion" can be quite different - from benevolently courteous to uncompromising and orderly. Although the first option is realized more often, since any religion or religious figure will not miss the opportunity, as noted above, "to extend its influence on the sphere of political relations, culture and education". At the same time, the political power builds relations in such a way as to prevent the religious power from increasing on the masses, keeping its position within reasonable boundaries. By "reasonable boundaries" we mean such a state of state-confessional relations that meet the expectations of the state political power.

According to A. Sultangalieva, in Kazakhstan the phenomenon of "official

Islam" is a product of the Soviet policy of control over religion, which ultimately turned religious structures into one of the quasi-state bodies for "religious affairs". The Spiritual Administration of Muslims of Kazakhstan (DUMK) in its structure was a copy of SADUM (Central Asian Spiritual Administration of Muslims of Central Asia and Kazakhstan), from which it was separated. Structures of organized Islam are unofficially supported by the authorities, and this model of relations between the state and Islam is widespread in many post-Soviet countries. In the literature, this trend is called "co-optation" of organized Islam by the state. The Mufti usually accompanies the country's top leadership at official events, and the state finances a number of projects related to the activities of the DUMK, such as grants for religious education. Local state bodies view assistance to the Muftiyat as one of their responsibilities. In their current form, the institutions of organized Islam have actually become "departments" of the state authorities to work in the religious sphere [16, p. 126-127]. The most striking evidence of this is the growth in the number of mosques throughout the country. Today there are 2415 mosques in Kazakhstan against 68 in 1991[1] . At the same time, there are cases when the construction of mosques in sparsely populated areas faces the problem of providing trained religious personnel.

At a meeting with representatives of the Spiritual Administration of Muslims of Kazakhstan, the Head of State Nursultan Nazarbayev called on the new leadership of the DUMK to strengthen the traditions of mutual understanding, tolerance and religious tolerance together with other religious associations. "In addition, it is necessary to continue further work on strengthening inter-ethnic and inter-confessional harmony"[*] [†] . "Islam should always do good. A Muslim should not harm anyone by word or deed, Islam calls

---

[1] Religious associations in Kazakhstan. Reference book. "Center for Research of Religious Problems" of the Department of Religious Affairs of the Akimat of Kostanay region. Kostanaipolygraphy LLP, p. 11

[†] Nazarbayev N.A. Adherence to Islam should not be a tribute to fashion [Electronic resource] / N.A. Nazarbayev // nur.kz: network edition // URL: http://www.nur.kz/250904.html (date of access:18.01.2016)

for unity, not division, calls for calm and peace"[‡] - the President noted.

As we can see, the state, having assumed the duty of guardianship of religion, no longer looks at it as an element of private life, but brings it into the sphere of politics.

Various methods of influence are used here, and religion, actively participates in the realization of "earthly affairs".

Hence, it is legitimate to conclude that some functions of the state, for example, the function of integration of society, are moving into the religious sphere, and as a consequence, Islam is being formalized as a tacit element of the political system. Integration, as noted above, is a constitutive property of religion itself. However, in the context of state-confessional relations, it acquires new shades, among which, for example, integration in order to counter destructive cults within Islam. This is a very complex task, where religion must combine religious integration (with the aim of saving souls) and worldly integration, with the aim of saving the whole society and the state. Today, the DUMK together with the Ministry of Religious Affairs and Civil Society work in close tandem to counter religious extremism and promote the ideas of secularism.

2. *Conflict sub-model.* We believe that here we should focus on the development of state-confessional relations in the context of a particular political regime. In particular, this option is actualized in the conditions of political transit in the post-Soviet countries that have embarked on the path of democratization.

In one of her works, Alma Sultangalieva notes that Central Asian countries have adopted laws that control, to a greater or lesser extent, the activities of religious associations. In many respects, this is a continuation of the Soviet policy of dominating prohibitive procedures [Cited in 14, p. 275]. One of the important political events that caused great resonance was the adoption by the Majilis of Kazakhstan on September 22, 2011 of the bill "On Religious Activity and Religious Associations", Article 7 of which "caused resistance even among

[‡] Nazarbayev N.A. Islam calls for unity [Electronic resource] / N.A. Nazarbayev // Zakon kz: network edition // URL: http://www.zakon.kz/4520976-n.nazarbaev-islam-prizyvaet-k-edinstvu.html (date of address: 18.01.2016)

representatives of traditional confessions" [Cited in 18, p. 275]. [Cited in 18, p. 276]. The demand for revision and direct disregard of the provisions of legislation in the field of religion carries a certain degree of conflict potential, and "any disobedience of religion to the authorities already gives it some political connotation" [1, p. 4]. [1 ,c. 4]. Analyzing the attitude of official Islam to the new law, we can conclude that in some situations the positions of Muslim figures take a dysfunctional character in relation to the state policy in the sphere of religion. This situation has a negative impact both on the image of the state and on the image of DUMK.

— **a model of religious-political radicalism , camouflaged by Islam.**

In modern science, radicalism (from Late Latin radicalis - radical, Latin radix - root) is understood as:

— socio-political ideas and actions aimed at decisively changing existing institutions;

— accelerated, more decisive development of any process, phenomenon, etc. [19];

— radicalism implies a break with recognized tradition.

It is used within moderate reformist movements. This term is often used as a synonym in the academic literature on the problems of Islamism, along with such terms as politicization of Islam, extremism, terrorism.

In this article, we understand radicalization of Islam as "a political process based on the ideological doctrine of radical Islam (Islamism), which involves the implementation of differentiated specific political practices - from the implementation of the so-called "Islamic call" (moderate radicalism) to the total conduct of subversive and terrorist actions against the "enemies of Islam", justifying it by the "struggle for faith" - jihad - in order to build a "struggle for faith" (jihad). (moderate radicalism) to total subversive and terrorist actions against the "enemies of Islam", justifying it with the "struggle for faith" - jihad, in order to build an Islamic state and the introduction of Sharia law (ultra-radicalism)" [3]. [3].

Experts believe that the extremist metamorphosis in Kazakhstan occurred with the emergence of Salafism in our country. This trend promotes an alternative ideology to traditional Islam, seeks to disunite and divide believers along confessional lines, and criticizes existing social orders and moral norms. At the same time, Salafism is not homogeneous in its essence, and has a lot of both similar and radically different views [13, p. 31]. Consequently, the attitude to politics and manifestation of the political in Salafism are also heterogeneous.

In this model, we propose to distinguish the following sub-models:

1 - fundamentalist sub-model.

To characterize it, let us turn to the definition of fundamentalism in Islam proposed by R. Landa. In his opinion, fundamentalism is, first of all, an invariant of religious ideology, not a practice, much less a political one. It "can be defined as an ideological utopia and at the same time as an attempt to express the uniqueness of Islamic civilization" and as a form of "self-affirmation of Islam as a socio-cultural system". How and for what purposes Islamists use this ideology is another matter. Nevertheless, it seems quite reasonable the point of view expressed by academician E.M. Primakov, an Arabist-Eastern scholar familiar with Islamic studies, who stated in the fall of 1996 that "we do not equate Islamic fundamentalism and Islamic extremism" [8, p. 42]. [8, c. 42]. The main reason for the popularity of Salafism lies in the fact that it was a reaction to the limitations of traditional Islam, its inability to provide answers to acute life, including political issues. The emergence of Salafism was inevitable, and Islamic migration contributed to it [9].

Fundamentalism is the boundary beyond which religion turns into a kind of political ideology. Although many scholars, both domestic and foreign, believe that Islam is essentially an ideology. We do not quite agree with this opinion. The question of the relationship between religion and ideology is a vast topic, and in order to briefly show our position we consider it appropriate to refer to the opinion of A. A. K. Kovalev.

Kosichenko, who states the following: "The relationship of man with God as the central content and essence of religion takes it out of a number of ideologies and places it above them. All ideologies build horizontal links between its subjects, even in totalitarian ideologies, and religion, by definition, is a vertical "God - man", and the presence of God in this vertical makes religion a process of spiritual growth of man to God, which is much more than any ideology" [7, p. 82]. [7, c. 82].

To this sub-model we refer to those representatives of Islam who are called "sympathizers. "Sympathizers" are citizens who were (or are - author's note) members of the jamagat (radicalization - author's note), materially and intellectually helping its other members, but have no criminal intentions§ . In turn, these people are the main conductors of radical ideology, voluntary missionaries who have a serious impact on the political culture of the population, in the broadest sense. Fundamentalism is the basis for the emergence of religious and political extremism and terrorism, which represent the following sub-model.

2 - religious and political extremism and terrorism.

Such (extreme, radical) form of politicization of religion is associated primarily with the deliberate use of political violence and is aimed at destabilizing or destroying the basic political structures of a particular society, overthrowing the constitutional order [13, p. 31]. The ideology developed by fundamentalists here is not just disseminated and popularized, but is put into practice.

According to E. Karin, if in the early 2000s the terrorist threat in Central Asia was largely associated with the activities of such large associations as the IMU (Islamic Movement of Uzbekistan - author) and SID (Islamic Jihad Union - author), then in the period 2010-2013 small ethnic terrorist groups tied to a particular country began to appear. The emergence of these groups gave some experts reason to talk about the institutionalization of the threat of terrorism in

§ Evolution of an Islamist in Kazakhstan - from an ordinary believer to a terrorist (Analytical report on the results of sociological research) [Text] / Center for Security Programs and Public Foundation "Center for Social and Political Studies "Strategy". Almaty, 2013. 13 c.

the republics [6, p. 163]. The activities of all known pro-Islamic extremist organizations in Kazakhstan are prohibited by law. Religious extremists quickly master methods of conspiracy and are incorporated into an extensive network based on hierarchical levels and small cells of ordinary members at the lower level.

The dynamics of growth of the population's religiosity led to an increase in the ethno-confessional factor, within which religion began to perform the functions of an instrument of social consolidation and even political mobilization [2, p. 69].

"Mosaic" religious palette complicates the spiritual life of the country, gives rise to alarming symptoms caused by the growing susceptibility of the population to religious influence, expansion of social functions of religious associations, strengthening of missionary and ideological activities in Kazakhstan of charitable organizations. These factors can lead to the worldview polarization of the population, on the one hand, and an attempt to unify the worldview - on the other hand; strengthening the struggle between traditionalists and modernists; between tolerant believers and supporters of fanaticism and extremism [2, p. 75]. Inter- and intra-confessional competition does not just affects and affects society, but becomes an integral part of the socio-political process and has an impact on political culture.

Based on the above, we propose the following definition of the politicization of Islam, reflecting the specifics of this process in some post-Soviet countries, and in Kazakhstan, in particular. Politicization of Islam is a phenomenon characterized by counter processes, determined on the one hand by the activities of institutions of state political power, on the other hand by Islamic organizations, the main result of which is the actualization of political meanings in Islamic theory and practice, and as a consequence, the spread of Islamic influence on all spheres of society.

1. Aktaulova B., Sapanova S. On the politicization of Islam in Central Asia: essence, causes, consequences [Text] / B. Aktaulova, S. Sapanova // Bulletin of KazNU. Series of Oriental Studies. 2012. №1 (58). C. 3-8.

2. Vilkovski D. Arab-Islamic organizations in modern Kazakhstan: external influence on Islamic revival: Monograph [Text] / D. Vilkovski. Astana - Almaty: IMEP at the Foundation of the First President, 2014. 192 c.

3. Hajibekov R.G. Internal factors of influence on the processes of politicization of Islam in the Russian Federation. - Author's thesis ... Cand. of political sciences / R.G. Gadjibekov; Ros. akad. nar. khozyaistva i gosudarstvennosti servis under the President of the Russian Federation. - Rostov-on-Don, 2013. [Electronic resource] // DSLIB.NET: Bibl. of dissertations. URL: http://www.dslib.net/polit-instituty/vnutrennie-faktory-vlijanija-na-processy- politizacii-i-i-radikalizacii-islama-v.html (date of reference: 28.01.2015).

4. Danilov, M.V. Models of politicization of public relations [Text] / M.V. Danilov // Izvestiya Sarat. un-ta. Nov. ser. Ser. Sociology. Politologiya. 2014. T. 14, vol. 1. P. 80-83;

5. Drinova, E.M. Confessional geopolitics and processes of politicization of religion [Text] / E.M. Drinova // Bulletin of Volgograd State University. Series 7: Philosophy. Sociology and social technologies. 2008. № 2. C. 2014-2018.

6. Karin E. "Soldiers of the Caliphate": Myths and reality. [Text] / E. Karin. Almaty, 2014. 173 c.

7. Kosichenko A.G. Religious consciousness of Kazakhstanis and the problems of improving religious policy in the Republic of Kazakhstan // Kazakhstan, aspiring to the future: materials of the scientific-practical conference (Almaty, December 10, 2013) / Ed. by B.K. Sultanov. - Almaty: KISI under the President of the Republic of Kazakhstan, 2013. - C. 71-83.

8. Landa R.G. Political Islam: preliminary results. Scientific edition. [Text] / R.G. Landa. Moscow: Institute of Middle East, 2005. 286 c.

9. Malashenko A., Working Materials of the Program "Religion, Society and Security" [Electronic resource] // URL: http://carnegie.ru/2015/04/23/ru-

59854/i7pc (date of address: 31.10.2016).

10. Mirzakhanov D.G. Features of politicization of the Islamic community of Dagestan at the present stage. - Author's dissertation ... ... Cand. of philos. sciences / D.G. Mirzakhanov; Dagestan State University. - Makhachkala, 2005. [Electronic resource] // URL: http://www.dissercat.com/content/osobennosti-politizatsii-islamskoi-obshchiny-dagestana-na-sovremennom-etape (date circulation: 18.01.2016).

11. Pavlovnin, M.S. Interaction of religion and politics in the modern political space [Text] / M.S. Pavlovnin // Bulletin of Tomsk State University. 2012. № 359. C. 44-46.

12. Panarin A.S. Philosophy of Politics. Textbook for political science faculties and humanitarian universities [Text] / A.S. Panarin. Moscow: New School, 1996. 424 c.

13. Counteraction to religious extremism and terrorist activity in Kazakhstan (methodological manual) [Text] / KSU "Center for Research of Religious Problems" of the Department of Religious Affairs of the Akimat of Kostanay region. Executor: Public Association "Sotsium & Ya". - Kostanay, 2015: - 80 p.

14. Raimon A. Stages in the Development of Sociological Thought [Text] / A. Raimon. ed. and preface by P.S. Gurevich. Moscow: Publishing Group "Progress" - "Politics", 1992. 608 c.

15. Strizoe, A.L. Politics and society: socio-philosophical aspects of interaction [Text] / A.L. Strizoe. Volgograd: Izd-v Volgograd State University, 1999. 319 c.

16. Sultangalieva A.K. "Return of Islam" in Kazakhstan [Text] / A.K. Sultangalieva. Almaty: Fund "Altynbek Sarsenbayuly", 2012. 170 c.

17. Teryoshina, E.A. The concept of politicization of religion [Text] / E.A. Teryoshina // Scientific Notes of Kazan University. Humanities. 2012. Vol. 154, Book 1. P. 254-260.

18. Tuiganov, M.S. Trends of revival of Islam in Kazakhstan in the context of

democratic transformations [Text] / M.S. Tuiganov // Fates of national cultures in the context of globalization: Proceedings of the III Intern. scientific conference - Chelyabinsk, 2015. - C. 273-277.

19. Encyclopedic Dictionary. Radicalization [Electronic resource] / Academician: electronic dictionary// . URL:http://dic.academic.ru/dic.nsf/es/137391/радикализация(date of address : 27.01.2015 г.).

References

1. Aktaulova B., Sapanova S.O (2012) *Vestnik KazNU. Serija vostokovedenia,* no. 1 (58), pp. 3-8 [in Rus].

2. Vil'kovski D. (2014) Arabo-islamskie organizacii v sovremennom Kazahstane: vneshnee vlijanie na islamskoe vozrozhdenie, Astana - Almaty, IMJeP pri Fonde Pervogo Prezidenta, 192 p [in Rus].

3. Gadzhibekov R.G. (2013) DSLIB.NET: Bibl. Dissertacij, available at: http://www.dslib.net/polit-instituty/vnutrennie-faktory-vlijanija-na-processy-politizacii-i-i-radikalizacii-islama-v.html (accessed 28.01.2015 g.) [in Rus].

4. Danilov M.V. (2014) *Izvestiya Saratovskogo universiteta. Novaya seriya. Seriya Sotsiologiya. Politologiya,* T. 14, no. 1, pp. 80-83 [in Rus].

5. Drinova E.M. (2008) *Vestnik Volgogradskogo gosudarstvennogo universiteta. Serija 7: Filosofija. Sociologija i social'nye tehnologii,* no. 2, pp. 2014-2018 [in Rus].

6. Karin E. (2014) "Soldaty Halifata": Mify i real'nost', Almaty, 173 p. [in Rus].

7. Kosichenko A.G. (2013) Religioznoe soznanie kazahstancev i problemy sovershenstvovanija religioznoj politiki v Respublike Kazahstan [Text] // *Sostojavshijsja Kazahstan, ustremlennyj v budushhee: materialy nauch.-*

praktich. konf., pp 71-83.

8. Landa R.G. (2005) Politicheskij islam: predvaritel'nye itogi, Moskva: Institut Blizhnego Vostoka, 286 p. [in Rus].

9. Malashenko A., Rabochie materialyi Programmyi "Religiya, obschestvo i bezopasnost", available at: http://carnegie.ru/2015/04/23/ru-59854/i7pc (accessed 31.10.2016) [in Rus].

10. Mirzahanov D.G. (2005) DISSERCAT.COM: Jelektronnaja biblioteka dissertacij, available at: http://www.dissercat.com/content/osobennosti-politizatsii-islamskoi- obshchiny-dagestana-na-sovremennom-etape (accessed 18.01.2016) [in Rus].

11. Pavlovnin M. S. (2012) *Vestnik Tomskogo gosudarstvennogo universiteta,* no. 359, pp. 44-46 [in Rus].

12. Panarin A.S. (1996) Filosofija politiki, Moscow, Novaja shkola, 424 p. [in Rus].

13. Protivodejstvie religioznomu jekstremizmu i terroristicheskoj dejatel'nosti v Kazahstane (metodicheskoe posobie) (2015) KGU "Centr issledovanij religioznyh problem" Upravlenija po delam religij akimata Kostanajskoj oblasti. Ispolnitel': Obshhestvennoe ob#edinenie "Socium & Ja", Kostanaj, 80 p. [in Rus].

14. Rajmon A. (1992) Jetapy razvitija sociologicheskoj myslishh. red. i predisl. P.S. Gurevicha, Moscow, Izdatel'skaja gruppa "Progress" - "Politika", 608 p. [in Rus].

15. Strizoe A.L. (1999) Politika i obshhestvo: social'no-filosofskie aspekty vzaimodejstvija, Volgograd, Izd-vo Volgogradskogo gosudarstvennogo universiteta, 319 p. [in Rus].

16. Sultangalieva A.K. (2012) "Vozvrashhenie islama" v Kazahstan, Almaty, Fond "Altynbeka Sarsenbajeva", 170 p. [in Rus].

17. Terjoshina E.A. (2012) Ponjatie politizacii religii [Tekst] / E.A. Terjoshina // *Uchenye zapiski Kazanskogo universiteta. Gumanitarnye nauki*. Tom 154, kn. 1, pp. 254 - 260 [in Rus].

18. Tujganov M.S. (2015) *Sud'by nacional'nyh kul'tur v uslovijah globalizacii: sbornik materialov III Mezhdunar. nauch. Konf,* Cheljabinsk, pp. 273-277.

19. Jenciklopedicheskij slovar'. Radikalizacija. Akademik: jelektronnyj slovar', available at: http://dic.academic.ru/dic.nsf/es/137391/radikalizacija (accessed 27.01.2015) [in Rus].

IDENTITY CRISIS AS A CONDITION FOR RADICALIZATION OF KAZAKHSTANI YOUTH

Abstract: The article shows the problem of identity of Kazakhstani youth in modern conditions of revival of religion. The author identifies the main determinants of radicalization of youth in the context of identity crisis.

Keywords: identity, identity crisis, radicalization, dominant identity.

Young people have always been the part of society on which all hopes for the future development of the state are pinned. Kazakhstan's independence has opened up many options for socio-economic and socio-political development.

Today's youth policy in Kazakhstan pays great attention to the inclusion of the young generation of Kazakhstanis in social processes. The main means are, first of all, primary social institutions (education system), as well as public, socio-political, non-governmental organizations, youth forums, events at the republican and regional levels.

Nevertheless, against the background of active development of youth policy, there are still problems related to the self-determination of young people in the issues of life attitudes, moral principles, values, and as a consequence, spiritual security. A special role in these processes is played by the phenomenon of identity, which in recent years has been actualized in socio-humanitarian theory and practice.

Identity is a category of socio-humanitarian sciences (psychology, social philosophy, cultural anthropology, social psychology and

identity is a term used to describe individuals and groups as relatively stable, "identical to themselves" entities. Identity is not a property (i.e. something inherent in an individual from the beginning), but an attitude. It is formed, fixed

(or, on the contrary , redefined),

is transformed) only in the course of social interaction. In the strict sense of the word, identity can be attributed only to individuals, since only individuals possess the quality of subjectivity and, accordingly, are capable of attributing or not attributing certain meanings to themselves. It is only permissible to attribute identity to groups in a figurative, metaphorical sense..... In the structure of identity we can distinguish "individual" and "social" levels. If personal identity is a set of characteristics that give an individual the quality of uniqueness, then social identity is the result of identification (identification) of an individual with the expectations and norms of his social environment [1]. Overcoming the identity crisis is painless in homogeneous communities (in case of any shocks). However, Kazakhstan society does not belong to such communities. Multinationality and polyconfessionality are "historical satellites" of our social reality. The collapse of the Soviet Union led to a deep crisis of identity, both at the personal and social level. The consequences of this crisis are manifested in all spheres of life - from everyday situations to situations of national importance.

For many "transnational organizations" (official and unofficial), independent Kazakhstan has become an object for the implementation of various kinds of social projects. Pseudo-religious organizations play a special role among them.

It should be noted that the resulting "spiritual vacuum", which was one of the determinants of the identity crisis, contributed to the formation of a new identity structure for the entire Kazakhstani society, and for young people in particular.

"Spiritual vacuum", was filled with new content, mostly imported from other cultures. First of all, this is Western liberal consumer culture and Eastern traditional Islamic culture, mainly Arab. Their rapid spread and "melting" into the structure of identity was due to a number of reasons. First of all, globalization processes, in which our country was actively involved. Secondly, liberal legislation at the dawn of independence in the sphere of cultural and spiritual construction, including religious. Here we can also include the lack of deep understanding of the essence of the process of mutual influence and mutual enrichment of cultures in the context of globalization, and, as a consequence, the transformation of the "dialogue of cultures" into an actual "monologue", where our society acted as an object of manipulation by the "West and East". And finally, the presentability of the subjects of the "monologue" as a result of mature and successful marketing that meets the requirements of the modern market (in the broadest sense of the word).

Our youth found themselves in the embrace of this "monologue", actually zombified by it. This is where the crisis of identity came to light.

However, there were positive sides to the formation of identity. Starting from the late 1990s, new elements of Kazakhstani civic consciousness began to penetrate into the structure of identity. The ideological role in this was played by program documents, such as "Kazakhstan-2030", and the subsequent projects on modernization of all spheres of society, including youth issues. But the decisive role was played by economic growth, improvement of the welfare of Kazakhstanis, stable domestic political situation, which stands out brightly against the background of flaring "color revolutions" in post-Soviet countries.

Consequently, there is a contradictory situation in the formation of the identity of Kazakhstani youth, which was characterized, on the one hand, by an active influence from the outside, and on the other hand, by internal "reproduction
ideas" as the supposed foundations of the future Kazakhstani identity, which in turn predetermined its instability.

Under these conditions, a new model of identity of Kazakhstani youth is being built, which is undergoing complex processes. Metamorphoses are taking place at the personal level, which can be summarized by the formula proposed by S.S. Zagrebina. She notes that the socio-cultural characteristics of the individual (gender, age, nationality, citizenship, social status, religious affiliation, etc.) are in a state of internal conflict, on the one hand, and strong external pressure, on the other. A phenomenon emerges that can be called "dominant identity", when one of the forms of self-identification of a person becomes determinant, to the detriment of other components of the personality. One example is the actualization of gender identity in the European political and cultural space. Another example is the actualization of confessional identity among representatives of radical Islam in different parts of the world. The reasons for the crisis of identity on a global scale are seen in the deepening process of globalization, which unifies cultural differences. In these conditions, ethnic or confessional identity becomes the basis of resistance to aggressive unification and standardization in modern civilization [Cited in 2, pp. 92-93].

A retrospective analysis of youth involvement in radical pseudo-religious organizations shows that the identity crisis was one of the determinants of this process. From the point of view of identity, the following main determinants of this process can be distinguished:

1. The objective process of searching for self-identification as a psychosocial feature of young people against the background of unstable and not fully formed value socio-cultural orientations of Kazakhstan society;
2. Active proselytizing activity of pseudo-religious organizations, based on negative identification, where the comparative approach is used - "how our faith is better than others" or "how other faiths are worse than ours". This, it should be recalled, is the beginning of what we call intolerant relations, which later transforms into various forms of xenophobia;
3. A high level of marginalization of young people as a consequence of the identity crisis, due to the decline in education or its formalism with the concomitant devaluation of knowledge, the rapid pace of urbanization;
4. Lack of integrative national ideas. There were proposals and attempts to form them, but the issue was finally resolved in 2014, when the President of the country, the Leader of the Nation N. Nazarbayev voiced the idea of "Mzgilik El", "the national idea of our all-Kazakhstan home, the dream of our ancestors". The announcement of the patriotic act is the beginning of a long journey, its quality and success will depend on the main markers of socio-

political and socio-economic development.

Another important point in the radicalization of young people is the role of communication. As V.I. Ermakov notes, the most important basis for the choice that each person makes in the process of self-identification is the communicative reality, when the main characteristics of the individual are revealed in his or her speech behavior. This is possible if the personality itself maintains an invariant in all manifestations (dimensions) of identity: identity as identity; identity as self; narrative identity; identity as authenticity [Ibid., p. 91]. It is known that youth recruitment is carried out by well-trained specialists from radical pseudo-religious organizations. They have a rich experience of harmonious interweaving into the youth communicative environment. Moreover, many of them are themselves representatives of Kazakhstani youth. Their ability to transform and influence and then control the behavior of new adherents through specially selected words, slogans and speech combinations from different languages, subcultures, sometimes amaze the imagination of the most famous experts in the field of extremism prevention, or experienced theologians.

Thus, it can be stated that the identity crisis has become an important condition in the process of radicalization of Kazakhstani youth. The state needs to pay special attention to the qualitative development of integrative ideas, ideology and their realization within the framework of youth policy. In this regard, it should be noted the adoption of the Patriotic Act "Mzgilik El" on April 26, 2016 during the XXIV session of the Assembly of the People of Kazakhstan "Independence. Concord. Nation of a united future". The content of the Patriotic Act is represented by "seven inviolable foundations", penetrating all spheres of everyday life, be it education, science, culture, industry, agriculture. Society in turn should consciously approach the issue of ideological and ideological construction in Kazakhstan, because all efforts are aimed at the formation of a new Kazakhstani identity, which will be able to resist all manifestations of destructiveness and xenophobia.

Literature

1. New Philosophical Encyclopedia: In 4 vol. M.: Mysl. Edited by V. S. Støpin. 2001. *[Electronic resource]. URL:* http://dic.academic.ru/dic.nsf/enc_philosophy/419/ *(date of address 13.02.2016)*;
2. Borisov S.V. Modern man in search of identity (based on the materials of the interdisciplinary scientific symposium) // Sotsium i vlast 2014. № 6. C. 90-94.

"ISLAMIC STATE" AND DOMESTIC POLITICAL SECURITY IN KAZAKHSTAN

Abstract: The article is devoted to the issues of internal political security of Kazakhstan and threats coming from the so-called "Islamic State". The author shows the general logic of spreading in the world, and penetration of destructive religious movements in this or that country through the term "transgressive character of destructive religious movements".

Keywords: "Islamic State", internal political security, transgressive nature of destructive religious movements.

"Go, Muslims, for your country. Yes, because it is your country. Forward, because Syria does not belong to the Syrians and Iraq does not belong to the Iraqis," on June 28, 2014, the first day of Ramadan, Abu Bakr al-Baghdadi, by then Caliph Ibrahim, announced the end of ISIS (Islamic State of Iraq and the Levant) and the birth of the Islamic State. He was broadcasting from the pulpit of the Great Mosque of al-Nuri in Mosul, a city captured a few days earlier by its militants. An Iraqi by birth, al-Baghdadi abolished citizenship. In his view, there were no longer the peoples of the Fertile Crescent, nor the peoples of the rest of the world. Everything had been replaced by the Islamic State. Moreover, all mankind could henceforth be divided into two "camps". The first was "the camp of Muslims and mujahideen [holy warriors]," and the second was "the camp of Jews, crusaders and their allies" [1, p. 23]. [1, c. 23].

The horrors of everyday life, which are covered by the Middle East for Kazakhstanis are not something vague and elusive. For the first time Kazakhstan directly faced the threat of terrorism in 2011 [2, p. 12]. Terrorism itself and its consequences, as the consequences of any negative social phenomenon can be "extinguished" in a stable domestic political, economic, social, psychological situation. However, the whole world unites around the threat of terrorism precisely because the metamorphosis associated with adaptation, and as a consequence, the amazing ability to survive, reincarnate, strike even the most prosperous countries make terrorism the most terrible threat to domestic and geopolitical security.

Probably, many will agree with the opinion that domestic political security has long been associated in the mass and individual consciousness with security from encroachments by religious terrorist organizations. The most dangerous among them is the "Islamic State".

At first, I would like to clarify the fact that, despite a certain experience of existence of destructive religious organizations in Kazakhstan, including extremist and terrorist (underground), their activities and influence on society have not been fully studied. There are some successes in analyzing the overall situation, but there are no studies, for example, on the dynamics of their socio-political activity on political culture in general, and political consciousness in particular.

For more than two decades, as a result of liberal religious policy, there has been a rather serious fragmentation of religious space, characterized by a deep penetration of religious cults, both in the public and private spheres of people's lives. The facts of emergence of new denominations on the territory of the Republic of Kazakhstan, from moderate ("Alya Ayat", "Ata Zholy", "Senim. Bilim. ©mir.") to radical terrorist ("Jund al-Khalifat" ("Soldiers of the Caliphate")) are a vivid evidence of this. That is, Kazakhstani society itself began to create "author's religious projects" that were "successful" not only inside the country, but also outside it. The religious space, which received real opportunities for self-realization and institutionalization, turned into a multilevel structure.

Despite this, most of the attacks , committed and prevented were "foreign projects."

Taking into account the above stated, we consider it appropriate to introduce into scientific circulation the term "Transgressive character of destructive religious movements", under which we will understand the ability of some destructive religious movements to transfer in time and space elements of aggression of personal and social character.

In this concept, the word "transgressive" is borrowed from ecology, where it denotes one source of environmental pollution, namely, pollution spreading to a certain territory from other regions. The term "transgressive" in ecology is consonant with the concept of "Transboundary transfer", which means the spread of pollutants with air flows over long distances - beyond the borders of the states, on the territory of which the sources of pollution are located [3]. The basis of both terms is the concept of transit (from Latin transitus - passage). In this case, we apply it not as traditionally in political science, where it is defined as "a gap (interval) between one political regime and another" [Cited in 4], but as "a transit". [Cited in 4], but we use its original meaning - passage, consonant with such concepts as movement, movement, transition, penetration.

In addition, the transgressive nature of destructive religious movements became one of the main reasons determining the process of politicization of religious movements, as well as the disintegration, disorientation and heterogeneity of the religious space in general and the Muslim space in particular. The bright prospects that the Muslim community of Kazakhstan associated with the "return of Islam" were not realized. In particular, if we talk about Islam as a whole, it has not yet become a factor of integration even for the Kazakh ethnos, not to mention the entire multi-ethnic Muslim community. Contradictions within the religious space, conflict of interests, competition can provoke a situation in which the political culture of participation will be largely predetermined by the religious culture of participation.

It should be noted that IS is a geopolitical project. The capture of Iraq and Syria "turned IS into a factor of the world agenda" [1, p. 7] [1, c. 7]. Kazakhstan according to ISIS plans should enter the state of Khorasan [5]. According to the latest report of the U.S. Counterterrorism Center, information about which was disseminated by Azattyk radio, about 1000 people from Kazakhstan have already taken up arms against terrorists.... Official bodies insist on the figure of 450 people [6]. Even 450 for 17 million people in Kazakhstan is a lot, if we take into account the fact that "the recruitment of group members is done either individually or in small groups of 2-3 people and according to a strictly practiced methodology" [2, p. 76]. [2, c. 76]. At the end of June 2015 in the West Kazakhstan region, a verdict was passed on one of the most high-profile cases related to international politics in Kazakhstan. Two Umarov brothers were sentenced to 7 and 8 years in prison, respectively, for "Propaganda of terrorism". According to the investigation, the Umarovs tried to recruit their co-religionists and relatives into the ranks of supporters of the terrorist group "Islamic State" by inducing them to engage in unlawful conversations in the kitchen [6]. This is the reality in which we live.

Thus, the "Islamic State" possessing real "energy" of transgressive destructive religious and ideological character has a certain mediated influence on political culture and consciousness through social communications. One of the main tasks of the scientific community is to deeply analyze how this influence occurs, what informal factors, hidden social phenomena can turn into a real threat to the domestic political security of Kazakhstan in the future.

Literature

1. Weiss M., Hassan Hassan Islamic State: The Army of Terror; Translated from English - M.: Alpina Non-Fiction, 2016. - 346 c.;
2. Karin E. Soldiers of the Caliphate: Myths and Reality. - Almaty, 2014. - 174 c.;
3. Encyclopedia of Ecology.[Electronic resource]. URL: http://dic.academic.ru/dic.nsf/ecolog/ (accessed 08.01.15).
4. Veitzel D. Democratic transit in Kyrgyzstan: problems and practical recommendations. [Electronic resource]. URL: http://www.easttime.ru/analytics/kyrgyzstan/demokraticheskii-

tranzit-v- kyrgyzstane-problemy-i-prakticheskie-rekomendatsii;

5. Idoyatova G. ISIS militants have extended their ambitions to create a single state to Central Asia. [Electronic resource]. URL: http://astanatv.kz/news/show/id/25354.html;
6. Polovinko V. One foot in ISIS. [Electronic resource]. URL: http://www.novayagazeta.ru/politics/69287.html.

Sociocultural Foundations of the Non-Religious (Non-Muslim) Character of Social Conflicts in the Political History of Kazakhstan

Abstract: The article analyzes the problem of the influence of the spread of Islam in the territory of Kazakhstan in the context of social conflicts in the nomadic society. The peculiarities of syncretism in nomadic Islam and the absence of religious (Islamic) rhetoric in the social conflicts taking place in the political history of Kazakhstan are analyzed.

Keywords: Islam, syncretism, social conflicts, terrorist campaign, the heroic pantheon of Kazakhs.

On the territory of Kazakhstan, Islam was first declared the state religion in the Karakhanid state (10th century), but the wide spread and strengthening of Islam belongs to the era of Mongol rule (13th - 15th centuries). Here experts distinguish three stages of introduction of Muslimity in the Golden Horde: under the Khan Berk, Khan Uzbek and under Emir Yedig. The analysis of literature shows that despite the declaration of Islam as the state religion on the territory of Kazakhstan it did not lead to mass Islamization of the entire nomadic population. It was mainly the political elite and urban population that became adherents of Muslimism. Let us pay attention to the interpretation of the perception of Islam in medieval Kazakhstan, proposed by Abuseitova M.H. and Sultanov T.I.: "To all appearances, in the XIIIXIV centuries the rulers of the Golden Horde showed complete tolerance and tolerance in matters of faith of their subjects. The nature of the religious tolerance of the Djuchids is described in a letter of a brother of the Order of Minorites, Johanka Vengra, who visited the Golden Horde in 1320. "For the Tatars, - he wrote to the head of the Order Baron Michael, - military power subjugated to themselves different tribes of Christian peoples, but allow them to still keep their law and faith, not caring or little caring about who holds what faith, so that in peaceful service, in the payment of taxes and fees and military campaigns they (subjects) did for their masters what they are obliged by the issued law"" [2, c. 269]. The peculiarity of the spread of Islam among nomadic tribes of Kazakhstan was that the Muslim doctrine was easily adapted to the national traditions and customs of the Kazakh people. Thus, we can say that the strengthening of the position of the Muslim religion in the region took place against the background of preserving the position and certain harmonization with pagan beliefs. The so-called religious syncretism was formed, when the adherence to the Islamic doctrine was combined with the preservation of ancient pagan traditions in cult practice, the influence of animism, shamanism, ancestor worship remained noticeable [8]. The concept of religious syncretism can be found in many domestic and foreign authors. We believe that the process that eventually led to religious syncretism in Kazakhstan (and not only) will be appropriately designated by the term "territorialization", used by B. Andersen in the book "Imagined Communities". Here he attributes a special role to language. "As a result, ontological reality is comprehensible only through one single, privileged system of representation: the truth-language of ecclesiastical Latin, Koranic Arabic, or examplary Chinese. And as truth-languages, they are imbued with an impulse largely alien to nationalism: the impulse to conversion. By conversion I mean not so much the adoption of particular religious beliefs as an alchemical absorption. The barbarian becomes a subject of the "Middle State," the riffraff becomes a Muslim, and the Ilonggo becomes a Christian. The whole nature of human existence succumbs to sacralization" [3, c. 36]. Thus, Islam, having joined the nomadic civilization process became an element of the nomads' mentality, and as for its influence on social processes, it was superficial. Even in the most significant events in the life of man and society, Islam acted as a formal basis. Let us try to substantiate this thesis on the example of social conflicts.

The national liberation war of 1837-1847 under the leadership of Kenesary Kasymov can serve as a vivid illustration of the non-religious nature of social conflicts in the history of Kazakhstan. This war contributed to the rise of national self-consciousness, strengthening the national unity of Kazakhs.

In his book "Sultans Kenesary and Syzdyk" Ahmet Kenesarin writes: "Kenesary did not adhere to the slogan of "gazavat" - a holy war against infidels, so intensely propagandized at that time by Central Asian khans and clergy" [7 p. 8]. [7, c. 8]. The author contrasts not just Kazakhs, but Kazakh political elite with Central Asian khans and clergy, for whom "gazavat" was an ideological basis in the fight against colonialism. At the same time Kenesary retains his commitment to Islam, because "he gathers under his *green* banner all the offended" [7, p. 8] [7, c. 8]. In this situation, society was united by common goals, interests and needs, and the religious component did not turn into a political tool.

In the history of Kazakhstan, not a single social conflict or war with an external enemy has been motivated by Islam. Religion has never united the whole society for the realization of any historically significant projects. Of course, we do not aim to belittle the role of Islam in the ethno-political, cultural and historical formation of Kazakh society in general and the Kazakh ethnos in particular. Great thinkers of Kazakhstan, starting with Al-Farabi, were not just philosophers, but at the same time enlighteners from the big Muslim world. Shokan Ualikhanov, Abay and Shakarim, representatives of Kazakh national thought of the early XIX - XX centuries were not just based on the pillars of Islam, but were an integral part of Islamic culture. Shakhimardin writes: "Abay Kunanbaev and his religious teacher Ishan Auez were Sufi thinkers of the Naqshbandi persuasion. The author of the novel "Abai's Way" Mukhtar Auezov called himself a Naqshbandi. The very presence in the title of the concept of "path", one of the symbols of Sufism, speaks volumes" [4, c. 348]. Ibrai Altynsarin, an advocate of enlightenment in the steppe, an outstanding teacher, who opened the first public school in the steppe, was firmly committed to the religion of the Prophet Muhammad. His textbook on the basics of the Muslim faith can serve as evidence.

Consequently, religious relativism is also tendentious for Kazakh Islam, its syncretism. "Observers describing the life of Kazakhs at the end of the XIX century, usually emphasized that Islam was assimilated by Kazakhs superficially" [1, c. 91]. And this is more than eight centuries of Islam's melting into the steppes! As for tendentiousness, it is expressed not only in the preservation of ancient pagan cults in Kazakhs along with Islam, but in their predominance in the life of ordinary nomads and in the life of elites. Kazakhstan Islam as a synthesis of Kazakh and Islamic identity shows the real ways of dialog of different socio-cultural systems, the possibility of building a tolerant society on this basis.

Unfortunately, in recent years, destructive currents have begun to manifest themselves in the revival of Islam in Kazakhstan. The most dangerous of them are represented by extreme forms - extremism and terrorism

Every society that becomes the target of a massive terrorist attack responds in one way or another to the source of the intimidation. The nature of this response - conscious or unconscious, consolidated or fragmented, active or passive - is not just an illustration of society's attitude to something external, but an integral part of the events taking place. Society can dampen the activity of the source of intimidation, stimulate it, and contribute to its transformation into a different quality. The totality of "messages" addressed to society by the source of intimidation and the "responses" that it returns to it is a *terrorist campaign* - an intensive interaction between society and terrorists, dialog, exchange of acts of violence, political actions, ideological and emotional and figurative arguments [5, p. 77].

A terrorist campaign not only has its own theme, but also presents to society *the image of the terrorist, which is* formed by the source of intimidation in such a way that its main features are adequate to the theme of the campaign and maximally contribute to the course of the latter according to the terrorists' scenario. The "fighter for national happiness, defender of the disadvantaged", "true patriot fighting for national independence", "warrior in the name of Allah/Jesus, casting down the dark forces of evil", etc. have sought to intimidate some social, ethnic, confessional groups and even entire nations and states, relying on the support of other communities in the course of numerous terrorist campaigns that have taken place and are taking place around the world.

The nature of interaction between the source of intimidation (terrorist organization) and its object (terrorized society) is largely determined by the specifics of the emotional and imaginative experience of *the campaign theme by* society, as well as the degree of adequacy of the *terrorist image* to the mental state of society and its socio-cultural traditions. At the same time, a steadily upward development of terrorist campaigns is possible only if society *recognizes* the image of the terrorist and recognizes it as corresponding to the heroic pantheon fixed in the national culture.

Hence the great importance in most terrorist campaigns of the mechanisms of actualization of plots, themes and images of national cultures, which can be used by the sources of intimidation to sharply increase the influence of the intimidating image. Thus, the attack on Kizlyar by the detachment of Chechen terrorist S. Raduyev (1996). Raduyev (1996) is not only an act of terror against Russian society as a whole, but also the actualization of one of the authoritative stories of the heroic military tradition of the peoples of the Caucasus: the march on Kizlyar by the first imam of Chechnya and Dagestan, Gazi-Magomed, which served as an example of the "Kizlyar" campaign.

1831 signaled the beginning of the gazavat - the most acute phase of the Caucasian War. Appealing to local tradition, Raduyev sought sympathy primarily from the Caucasian audience, to whom he tried to set a "heroic" example by his actions [5, p. 78].

In his book "Soldiers of the Caliphate: Myths and Reality," Yerlan Karin analyzes the unfolding of the terrorist threat in Kazakhstan between 2002 and

2013.

For the first time Kazakhstan directly faced the threat of terrorism in 2011. Then, during the year, events related to the manifestation of terrorism occurred in various regions of the country and later received a wide public resonance. At first, the Kazakhstani authorities and special services did not recognize the events as terrorist acts and denied that those arrested or liquidated during special operations belonged to terrorist groups. However, the chain of various events clearly indicated that radical groups had become active in the country [6, p. 12]. We believe that the activation of radical groups in this case implies a very limited phenomenon on the scale of social space in general, and religious space in particular. One of the evidences of this is the fact that extremists failed to realize a simple, but very important task on the way to their goal - raising money. Of course, "sympathizers" appeared, but it was not enough. Extremists did not fit into the tolerant homogeneity of Kazakhstani society, and as a consequence, the cumulative effect they anticipated failed. Perhaps this is one of the reasons why the political elite of the country did not recognize these events as terrorist acts. But the most important thing is that religiously motivated extremism (of the Islamic persuasion), in no way reflects the emotional and imaginative experience of society of *the theme of the campaign,* as well as the degree of adequacy of the *image of the terrorist* to the mental state of society and its socio-cultural traditions.

The heroic pantheon of Kazakhs consists of heroes-batyrs, heroes-khans, hero-soldiers who gave their lives on the battlefields where military actions, self-sacrifice were directed against the external enemy invader, whether it was the Dzungars, whether it was the colonial policy of tsarism or fascist aggression.

Thus, the heroic history of Kazakhs was aimed primarily at preserving territorial integrity, the formed social order, it consolidated and strengthened the political system and the whole society. Radical Islam does not fit into the Kazakh heroic pantheon, it is an alien anti-social and anti-national product. Today Kazakh heroics is embodied in tolerance and is a continuation of this evolving tradition.

Literature

1. Abuov A.P., Smagulov E.M. Religions in Kazakhstan. - Kostanai: LLP "Kostanai Printing Yard". - 2011. - 255 c.
2. Abuseitova M.H. et al. History of Kazakhstan and Central Asia: Textbook - Almaty: Bilim, 2012. - 620 c.
3. Anderson B. Imagined Communities. Reflections on the origins and spread of nationalism / Translated from English by V. Nikolaev; Introductory article.
   C. Bankovskaya. - Moscow: "KANON-press-C", "Kuchkovo Pole", 2001. - 288c.
4. Artemiev A.I., Kolchigin S.Y., Tsepkova I.B. Religions in Kazakhstan: Chrestomathy in 2 parts. - Part 2. - Almaty: LLP "Antey", 2013. - 460 c.
5. Baranov A.S. Terrorism and civil martyrdom in the European political culture of New and Modern times // Social Sciences and Modernity. - №1. - 2004, c. 77 - 85.
6. Karin E. "Soldiers of the Caliphate": Myths and Reality. Almaty 2014. - 173 c.
7. Kenesarin A. Sultans Kenesary and Syzdyk: Biographical sketches. - Alma-Ata: Zhalyn, 1992, - 144 p.
8. Portal "History of Kazakhstan" http://e-history.kz/ru/contents/view/485, - [Electronic resource] (date of address 23.03.15).

TRENDS OF REVIVAL OF ISLAM IN KAZAKHSTAN IN THE CONTEXT OF DEMOCRATIC TRANSFORMATIONS

Abstract: The article deals with the contradictions in the revival of Islam, which Kazakhstan society faced after gaining independence. The peculiarities of the emergence of new problems in the conditions of globalization, democratic transformations and the current religious situation are shown. Special attention is paid to the law of the Republic of Kazakhstan "On Religious Activity and Religious Associations"

Keywords: revival of Islam, democracy, freedom of religion.

Freedom of conscience, or rather its realization in the Republic of Kazakhstan in the last decade has become a stumbling block in the framework of state-confessional relations. This was due to a number of closely interrelated reasons. First of all, it is necessary to note the powerful religious upsurge that began in the late Soviet period. The main "conductors" at that moment were internal forces led by traditional religious leaders and the same traditional views. The second factor is globalization. Undoubtedly, Kazakhstan has historically been and remains a part of Islamic culture, however, the penetration of new-fashioned Islamic ideas and trends and the negative phenomena that followed took the state by surprise.

Religion has an extremely uncertain status in the modern world. On the one hand, it is generally considered to be something high, important, significant - in any case, it is reckoned with, power structures flirt with it, fighters for justice appeal to it, hopes are pinned on it in many difficult situations, etc. on the other hand, religion is not really significant for most people, it is pushed into the sphere of abstract ideas, religious arguments are resorted to for opportunistic reasons, it is made responsible for extremism and terrorism; people are more interested in fashion and prices than in the norms of religious life [3, p. 122].

The revival of religion in Kazakhstan since independence has become one of the main "satellites" of the democratization process. One of the first measures to liberalize religious legislation was the abolition of the Council for Religious Affairs under the government of the Kazakh SSR. This body directly managed the activities of religious associations in the spirit of Soviet ideology and played an important role in the system of state administration. A logical continuation was the adoption of the law "On Freedom of Religion and Religious Associations". This law fully fit into the overall picture of democratic transformations.

In fact, even the very wording of the law "On Freedom of Religion and Religious Associations" spoke about the priorities that were set when it was created. In this case, there was no question of state regulation. This law with some changes was in force until September 22, 2011, when the Majilis approved the bill "On Religious Activity and Religious Associations", which meets the new realities [1, p. 19-20]. The new realities are primarily associated with the emerging threats to national security from representatives of Islamic extremist organizations.

Today, on the map of Islamic revival in Kazakhstan, two main directions can be distinguished - traditional Islam (the religion of the majority), which has been formed for centuries on the local cultural basis, and world Islam, which was formed during the years of independence and whose bearers are a small part of the population. Being a secular state, Kazakhstan has no special political instruments in relation to Islam. However, it can be stated that the tightening of legislation on religious associations is primarily due to threats to national security from Islam.

Since the adoption of the new Law on Religion in 2011, the question of the expediency of this step on the part of the state still raises many questions. Discussions continue about the reasons for the adoption of this law and the consequences for Kazakhstan. Moreover, both representatives of non-traditional and traditional religions express their criticism. The greatest resonance was caused by Article 7, which prohibits "conducting (performing) worship services, religious rites, ceremonies and (or) meetings, as well as missionary activities on the territory and in the buildings of state bodies and organizations" [2]. [2]. Alma Sultangalieva notes in this regard that the countries of Central Asia have adopted laws that control, to a greater or lesser extent, the activities of religious associations. In many respects, this is a continuation of the Soviet policy of dominating prohibitive procedures [7, p. 37]. We are also interested in the position of the U.S. official authorities, expressed on October 14, 2011 at the OSCE on the issue of the new Kazakhstani law on religion: "When governments excessively restrict freedom of religion and freedom of speech, or when societies do not take measures to promote tolerance and suppress discrimination on the basis of religious affiliation, they risk alienating believers and stimulating the activities of extremists" [6]. [6]. It is also possible to note the criticism of the state, expressed in the annual report of the U.S. Department of State on the situation in the field of religion in the world, which was published in May 2013. Regarding Kazakhstan, the report, which covers the situation in 200 countries, indicates that the 2011 law provides for strict mandatory requirements for the registration of missionaries and religious groups. The law prescribes grounds for refusing to grant religious groups official status [1, p. 18]. Official representatives of the Spiritual Administration of Muslims of Kazakhstan opposed some articles of the law.

The essence of discussions around the new law is whether the state should in principle try to regulate the religious sphere of society. Especially in connection with the fact that religion in Kazakhstan, according to the Constitution, is separated from the state, and the principle of freedom of conscience does not imply interference in the religious preferences of citizens. Hence, it is often concluded that the adoption of the new law is a step backward in the policy of development of the modern state, the rejection of liberal approaches of the early 1990s, that as a result the state and society received more problems in connection with its adoption than possible benefits [1, p. 19-20].

There is a certain logic in this, but there is also another logic when an open liberal environment, on the contrary, creates a favorable basis for the same extremists to spread their ideology. Especially when the activities of the latter are supported from outside a country, as is often the case with radical Islamists. An open system is always a competitive struggle of interests and ideologies. If society is able to withstand it, there are no problems. But if there is a risk of destabilization, the state must react in order to protect the way of life of the conservative majority of the population.

Previously we have talked about the relationship between the state and Islam in the context of democracy, but there is another plane - the relationship between Islam and other religions in the context of democracy. The main rhetoric is tied around "elitist confessions" represented by Sunni Islam and the Russian Orthodox Church and "non-elitist" represented by new religious movements belonging to different world religions. "Most government officials, Kazakhstani citizens, representatives of the Russian Orthodox Church and Sunni Islam publicly declare the idea of tolerance and the principle of freedom of conscience. However, these categories in their understanding have essentially intolerant meaning: only Sunni Islam, Russian Orthodoxy, Catholicism, Judaism and recently Lutherans should be honored with tolerant attitude and inter-confessional dialogue. They declare the activities of the majority of officially operating Protestant, neo-Protestant and so-called new religious associations to be "disastrous" for society. In relation to the "Protestant group" the intolerant consciousness dominates, bearing certain prejudices, biases, standards of thought and behavioral skills inherent in the undemocratic system" [8]. [8]. From a formal point of view, freedom of religion, including Protestants in Kazakhstan is the main priority of a democratic society.

However, freedom of religion also implies freedom of preaching, but the latter circumstance means that in fact we are talking about the freedom of competition between religious associations, which already creates a conflict situation between them. And this directly affects the interests of the state, which cannot ignore the interests of the majority of the population and those religions that are traditional for it [1, p. 23].

One can agree with the opinion of A. Kosichenko that "according to democratic norms and in accordance with the Law of the RK "On Freedom of Religion and Religious Associations" all confessions in Kazakhstan have equal rights. However, in fact, Islam and Orthodoxy play a greater importance in the life of Kazakh society in comparison with other confessions". Developing his thought, he points out: "as for the presence in Kazakhstan of the so-called new religious movements and the assessment of their influence on Kazakhstani society, it is quite obvious that these denominations must prove their positive impact on our society, and only then can they claim equal conditions for functioning in the Republic of Kazakhstan with Islam and Orthodoxy". This issue is directly related to the problem of state security and the discussion about the letter and spirit of the law regulating state policy in the field of religion goes beyond a purely theoretical dispute. This is a very practical issue [1, p. 25].

If we refer to the history of the issue, we recall that in 2005, additions were made to the law "On Freedom of Religion and Religious Associations". The law was supplemented with the preamble: "This law recognizes that the Republic of Kazakhstan is a democratic, secular state that respects the right of every people to freedom of belief, guarantees equality of citizens, regardless of their religion, recognizes the cultural and historical value of religions combined with the spiritual heritage of the peoples of Kazakhstan, and the importance of inter-confessional harmony, religious tolerance and respect for the religious beliefs of citizens." In fact, this preamble introduces a definition of "traditionalism" of religions into the law. "This experience was adopted from the Russian law, which also pays great attention to the importance of traditional religions. Although the preamble is not a norm of the law, it is significant for the interpretation of the whole law. Thus, the basis is laid for differentiation of confessions based on their contribution to the spiritual life of the people of Kazakhstan." Undoubtedly, the definition of "spiritual heritage of the peoples of Kazakhstan" is rather abstract, but it demonstrates, albeit restrained, but still, in general, a favorable attitude of the state [1, p. 28-29]. In fact, today the situation de facto represents the dichotomy "traditional - non-traditional", corresponding to the dichotomy "friend - enemy". At the same time, the state has assumed the responsibility of debunking the "non-traditional": the relevant legislation, the Agency for Religious Affairs, special units in the security forces, etc. In this regard, the modernization of the religious sphere in general, and the relationship between the state and Islam, which is based on the state control over religious associations is that Kazakhstan has chosen the strategy of "modeling" religion, based on the need to construct a national identity [7, p. 36]. We agree with the opinion of Zhanna

Onlasheva, who believes that the recognition of the historical role of Hanafi Islam in Kazakhstan should be used in public policy, taking into account the liberal nature of this mashab. Firstly, the Hanafi mashab is traditional for the territory of Kazakhstan for many centuries. Secondly, Hanafi Islam allows believers to live peacefully in a secular society. Thirdly, other directions of Islam, which oppose the secular structure of the state, other religions and Islamic movements, are spreading in Kazakhstan [5, p. 9].

A reasonable question arises - how justified is such activity of the state in addressing religious issues in a democracy? The answer to this question is formulated by the reality that has developed both in Kazakhstan, the region and the world as a whole. In this regard, at the enlarged meeting of the party "Nur Otan" on January 17, 2011, the President of the Republic of Kazakhstan Nursultan Nazarbayev noted: "We are a secular state, religion is separated from the state, but this does not mean that Kazakhstan should become a dumping ground for any religious movements. Today tens of thousands of various missionary organizations are working in Kazakhstan. We do not know their goals and objectives, and we should not allow such arbitrariness, complete freedom of what our country does not need" [4].

It follows from the above that at this stage the state cannot afford open religious competition. As for the Law of 2011, it is a kind of compromise solution between the most liberal approach, which is usually advocated by Western countries, and the most rigid version, which we see on the example of some countries formed in the former Soviet Union. Within the framework of the topic we have outlined, we think that P.I. Novgorodtsev's analogy regarding democracy, which is extrapolated to the situation in the state-confessional sector of Kazakhstan, will be appropriate here: "Since democracy is a system of political relativism, for which there is nothing absolute, which is ready to allow everything, any political possibility, any economic system, as long as it does not violate the beginning of freedom, - it is always a crossroads; no path is ordered here, no direction is forbidden here. The principle of relativity, of tolerance, of the widest admissions and recognitions prevails over all life, over all thought".

Literature

1. Akimbekov S. To the history and practice of religious policy in Kazakhstan // Kazakhstan in global processes. - 2013. - № 2. - C. 19-20.
2. Law of the Republic of Kazakhstan "On Religious Activity and Religious Associations" (with amendments and additions as of 29.09.2014).
3. Kosichenko A. Religion in global processes of modernity // Kazakhstan in global processes. - 2004. - № 1. - C. 122-131.
4. Nazarbayev N.A. It is necessary to suppress the activities of illegal religious movements in Kazakhstan - [Electronic resource]. - Mode of access: http://news.gazeta.kz/art.asp?aid=225950 (date of reference: 12.12.14).
5. Onlansheva Zh. The problem of implementation of the Law of the Republic of Kazakhstan "On religious activity and religious associations" // Kazakhstan in global processes. - 2013. - № 4. - C. 6-

12.
6. Rysaliev A. Toughening the policy of the Kazakhstani authorities with regard to religion [Electronic resource]. - Mode of access: http://thenews.kz/2011/11/10/965018.html (date of reference: 08.01.15).
7. Sultangalieva A. Religion and the state in modern Central Asia - challenges and prospects // Kazakhstan in global processes. - 2013. - №2. - C. 34-42.
8. Tsepkova I. B. Realities and myths of Kazakhstan religious tolerance [Electronic resource]. - Mode of access: http://religiopolis.org/documents/851-ib-tsepkova-realii-i-mify-kazahstanskoj-religioznoj-tolerantnosti-materiali-mezhdunarodnoj-nauchnoj-konferentsii-svoboda-religii-i-demokratii-starye-i-novye-vyzovy- kiev-avgust-2010.html (date of reference: 08.01.15).

HEROIC PANTHEON OF KAZAKHS VS. ACTIONS OF RELIGIOUSLY-MOTIVATED EXTREMISM IN THE INDEPENDENT KAZAKHSTAN

*Abstract:*The article is devoted to the heroic pantheon of Kazakhs as an element of modern mentality of Kazakh society. In the conditions of radicalization of Islam in Kazakhstan, the issue of its counteraction not only in force, but also in ideological terms is cautious. In this regard, the actualization of Kazakh heroics can become an important element in the formation of ideological immunity of society.

Keywords: heroic pantheon, religiously motivated extremism, terrorist campaign, enemy image.

During the years of Independence Kazakhstan has become different. Its spiritual content, emptied after the collapse of the USSR, began to be filled with new elements. History is developing in a spiral: the experiment with forced deportation of peoples to the territory of Kazakhstan from all corners of the Soviet Union was replaced by an involuntary experiment of religious expansion from all over the world. Experts call this phenomenon by various terms - "revival", "renaissance", "return" of religion. No matter how we treat these words, the religious space of our country is acquiring more and more clear forms in quantitative and qualitative format. The actualization of the topic is also connected with the problems of state-confessional character, the role of religion in general, and Islam in particular in the development of society and man that have arisen, especially in the last decade.

Kazakhstan has historically been and remains a part of Islamic culture, however, the penetration of new-fashioned Islamic ideas and trends and the negative phenomena that followed have created a problematic situation for society and the state.

Religion has an extremely uncertain status in the modern world. On the one hand, it is generally considered to be something high, important, significant - in any case, it is reckoned with, power structures flirt with it, fighters for justice appeal to it, hopes are pinned on it in many difficult situations, etc. on the other hand, religion is not really significant for most people, it is pushed into the sphere of abstract ideas, religious arguments are resorted to for opportunistic reasons, it is made responsible for extremism and terrorism; people are more interested in fashion and prices than in the norms of religious life [1, P. 122].

One of the relevant scientific and methodological approaches in studying the essence of religious extremism is communicative. It allows for a deeper understanding of the interests of the participants in the dialog.

Every society that becomes the target of a massive terrorist attack responds in one way or another to the source of the intimidation. The nature of this response - conscious or unconscious, consolidated or fragmented, active or passive - is not just an illustration of society's attitude to something external, but an integral part of the events taking place. Society can dampen the activity of the source of intimidation, stimulate it, and contribute to its transformation into a different quality. The totality of "messages" addressed to society by the source of intimidation, and the "responses" that it returns to it, is a *terrorist campaign* - an intensive interaction between society and terrorists, dialog, exchange of acts of violence, political actions, ideological and emotional and figurative arguments [2, P. 77].

A terrorist campaign not only has its own theme, but also presents to society the *image of the terrorist, which is* formed by the source of intimidation in such a way that its main features are adequate to the theme of the campaign and maximally contribute to the course of the latter according to the terrorists' scenario. The "fighter for national happiness, defender of the disadvantaged", "true patriot fighting for national independence", "warrior in the name of Allah/Jesus, casting down the dark forces of evil", etc. have sought to intimidate some social, ethnic, confessional groups and even entire nations and states, relying on the support of other communities in the course of numerous terrorist campaigns that have taken place and are taking place around the world.

The nature of interaction between the source of intimidation (terrorist organization) and its object (terrorized society) is largely determined by the specifics of the emotional and imaginative experience of *the campaign theme by* society, as well as the degree of adequacy of the *terrorist image* to the mental state of society and its socio-cultural traditions. At the same time, a steadily upward development of terrorist campaigns is possible only if society *recognizes* the image of the terrorist and recognizes it as corresponding to the heroic pantheon fixed in the national culture.

Hence the great importance in most terrorist campaigns of the mechanisms of actualization of plots, themes and images of national cultures, which can be used by the sources of intimidation to sharply increase the influence of the intimidating image. Thus, the attack on Kizlyar by the detachment of Chechen terrorist S. Raduyev (1996). Raduyev (1996) is not only an act of terror against Russian society as a whole, but also the actualization of one of the authoritative stories of the heroic military tradition of the peoples of the Caucasus: the march on Kizlyar by the first imam of Chechnya and Dagestan, Gazi-Magomed, which in 1831 served as a signal for the beginning of gazavat - the most acute phase of the Caucasian War. Appealing to local tradition, Raduyev sought sympathy primarily from the Caucasian audience, to whom he tried to set a "heroic" example by his actions [2, P. 78].

In his book "Soldiers of the Caliphate: Myths and Reality," Yerlan Karin analyzes the unfolding of the terrorist threat in Kazakhstan between 2002 and 2013.

For the first time Kazakhstan directly faced the threat of terrorism in 2011. Then, during the year, events related to the manifestation of terrorism occurred in various regions of the country and later received a wide public resonance. At first, the Kazakhstani authorities and special services did not recognize the events as terrorist acts and denied that those arrested or liquidated during special operations belonged to terrorist groups. However, the chain of various events clearly indicated that radical groups had become active in the country [3, P. 12]. We believe that the activation of radical groups in this case implies a very limited phenomenon on the scale of social space in general, and religious space in particular. One of the evidences of this is the fact that extremists failed to realize a simple, but very important task on the way to their goal - raising money. Of course, "sympathizers" appeared, but it was not enough. Extremists did not fit into the tolerant homogeneity of Kazakhstani society, and as a consequence, the cumulative effect they anticipated failed. Perhaps this is one of the reasons why the political elite of the country did not recognize these events as terrorist acts. But the most important thing is that religiously motivated extremism (of the Islamic persuasion), in no way reflects the emotional and imaginative experience of society of *the theme of the campaign,* as well as the degree of adequacy of the *image of the terrorist* to the mental state of society and its socio-cultural traditions.

The heroic pantheon of Kazakhs consists of heroes-batirs, hero-khans, hero-soldiers who gave their lives on the battlefields where military actions, self-sacrifice were directed against an external enemy invader, be it the Dzungars, Central Asian khanates, colonization of the Russian Empire or Nazi Germany. The victims of the December 1986 events did not aim at martyrdom or self-sacrifice. They became victims.

Thus, the heroic history of Kazakhs was aimed primarily at preserving territorial integrity, the formed social order, it consolidated and strengthened the political structure and the whole society. Radical Islam does not fit into the Kazakh heroic pantheon, it is an alien anti-social and anti-national product. Today, Kazakh heroics is embodied in tolerance and is a continuation of this evolving tradition.

Literature

1. Kosichenko A. Religion in global processes of modernity // Kazakhstan

in global processes. - 2004. - № 1. - C. 122-131.

2. Baranov A.S. Terrorism and civil martyrdom in the European political culture of New and Modern times // Social Sciences and Modernity. - №1. - 2004, c. 77 - 85.
3. Karin E. "Soldiers of the Caliphate": Myths and Reality. Almaty 2014. - 173 c.

THE ESTABLISHMENT OF THE SPIRITUAL ADMINISTRATION OF MUSLIMS OF KAZAKHSTAN AS A POLITICAL ORGANIZATION. SUBJECT

Abstract: This article deals with the issue of formation of the Spiritual Administration of Muslims of Kazakhstan (DUMK) as a political subject. In Kazakhstan, the renewal of Islam and religion in general, has a serious impact on the development of society and the state, and generates new processes in the religious environment. One of these processes is the process of transformation of DUMK into a political subject. Based on the analysis of the current situation, the main characteristics and features of this process are formulated.

Key words: Spiritual Administration of Muslims of Kaakhstan, subject, political subject, secular society.

In modern Kazakhstan the issues of influence of religious organizations, in particular Islam, on politics are becoming topical. Domestic and foreign political science is replenished with works in this area. Ambiguity in determining the essence, nature and role of Islam, in particular the Spiritual Administration of Muslims of Kazakhstan (hereinafter - DUMK) in the political life of Kazakhstan leads to the fact that in the scientific literature there are different approaches to its study, most of which need a detailed study. One of the serious problems is the ambiguity in the definition of the terms "politics" and "political subject". This causes a lot of controversy about whether Islam is politically active and whether it is a political subject.

In our study, we will use the substantive criterion of politics as well as the criterion of the political subject.

The problem of the political subject in science has a long history.

Traditionally, people, classes, social communities, and individuals are considered as political subjects in science. There are many approaches and points of view regarding the political subject.

In ancient philosophy, which is the basis of the theory of subjectivation, a person should be fully aware of every action aimed at his ethical education, which he produces on himself. I. Kant believed that man himself represents the subject and possesses all the attributes of the subject. Cognitively, he possesses a priori knowledge. To call himself a subject, he does not have to undergo any tests, to subject himself to ascesis, to test himself in order to confirm his proud title of man as a subject.

According to K. Marx, political subjects are classes with a special economic interest, united by their relationship to the means of production and the share of public wealth received. Modern society is a multilevel structure represented by many strata and many complex relationships between them. However, economic determinism cannot be denied completely, since economic interests lie behind many modern political actors.

In the theory of subjectivation, a person cannot be a subject in fact, but must strive to become one. Daily practice and constant work on oneself is what M. Foucault relies on when he talks about the subject.

T.A. Kulakova, studying the issues of involvement in publicity as an innovation of public administration in Russia, refers to the subjects of public policy as "the state and its institutions, business, civil society institutions, social, professional, ideological groups of the population, mass media" [1, p. 133]. [1, c. 133]. The author considers the involvement of the population by the state in public policy and their transformation into political subjects from the point of view of their activities in their interests and

functionality in public policy. At the same time, involving the population and public organizations in political processes, the state, most often tacitly, retains the right to patronize these organizations.

Consequently, a political subject is a *relatively* independent participant in the political process with its own interest in the sphere of politics

Islam in the history of Kazakhstan had a great influence on many processes. Islam positioned itself most clearly as a political subject in the early twentieth century. In March 1917, in the southern regions of Kazakhstan, which were part of the Turkestan Governor-General's Office, the Shura-i-Islami party was formed by clergy and clerically-minded intellectuals. M. Shokai, A. Kari, A. Temirbekov and others played an active role in the organization of the party. The ideology of "Shura-i-Islami" was based on three closely interrelated elements: ethnic cohesion of the Turkic-Muslim peoples in order to achieve their national self-determination; denial of the positive influence of "Russian revolutions"; and the establishment of a common ethnic and religious identity of the Turkic-Muslim nationalities. The central printed organ of the party was the newspaper "Shura-i-Islami". The party's political positions expressed the interests of the local wealthy strata of the population. It advocated national-religious autonomy of Turkestan within bourgeois Russia, supported the Turkestan Committee of the Provisional Government, and envisioned reforms in education and everyday life.

In June 2017, the Shura-i-Islami party split from the Shura-i-Ulema party, which was positioned as a counter-revolutionary pan-Islamist organization. It united the highest Muslim clergy, local feudal lords and the most reactionary part of the national bourgeoisie. At the congress of "Shura-i-Ulema" in Tashkent in September 1917, the delegates opposed the Soviets, demanded the separation of Turkestan from Russia and the unification of all Muslims in a single Muslim state under the aegis of Turkey, the establishment of branches of "Shura-i-Ulema" in all cities of the Turkestan region. At the 3rd Congress of Soviets of the region (November 1917) the Ulemists opposed the establishment of Soviet power in Turkestan, were among the organizers of the counter-revolutionary Kokand autonomy and the inspirers of the Basmachi. In the struggle against the Soviet power the Ulemists were in alliance with Russian White Guards and foreign imperialists. The Ulemists, headed by their leader lawyer S. Lapin, stood on the position of the Russian White Guards and foreign imperialists. Lapin stood on the position of "realization of the legitimate rights of Muslims to self-determination, built on purely Muslim principles and the principles of Sharia".

"Shura-i-Islami" and "Shura-i-Ulema" had the same national values, but different - political. In September 1917 at the Congress of Kazakh and Turkestan Muslims it was decided to unite "Shura-i-Islami" and "Shura-i-Ulema" and other national organizations into a single political party "Ittifok-i-Muslimin" ("Union of Muslims"). A resolution was adopted which put forward the idea of forming a Turkestan autonomy with a two-tier government within Russia under the name of Turkestan Federal Republic. In October, in violation of the unification agreement, the Shura-i-Islami and Shura-i-Ulema independently nominated candidates for the Constituent Assembly, each from their own party.

In early 1918, the Council of People's Commissars of Turkestan and local Soviets dissolved the Shura-i-Islami and Shura-i-Ulema parties for anti-Soviet activities [2].

Thus, even in the early twentieth century, Islam represented a real political force and acted as a subject of politics. Muslim parties tried to take responsibility for the entire state, had specific political claims, programs and actions. At the present stage, the transformation of Islam into a subject of politics is blocked by the secular form of the state, but this does not prevent Islam from acquiring political qualities.

The radical ideological transformations of the late 1980s and 1990s contributed to an increase in the number of Muslims (up to 72%) identifying themselves primarily with the DUMK. Islam acquired the status of an organization that has a serious impact on public consciousness, on all spheres of public life, including political life.

State political structures, parties and public organizations are increasingly interested in the opinions and activities of Muslim leaders on acutely topical issues. However, in the conditions of an open society and confessional pluralism within Islam, a number of currents emerge that do not recognize the DUMK as their leader, which forms a diverse and ambiguous relationship.

As already noted, the majority of Muslims, predominantly the indigenous population, identify themselves with the Spiritual Administration of Muslims of Kazakhstan, which has become the main conductor of the legitimization of Islam. But at the same time, according to official data, among Muslims there are up to 15 thousand representatives of the Salafi direction [3], although in 2013 there were only 495 people in 24 radical Salafi communities [4]. This rapid growth is due to the confessional conversion of representatives of traditional Islam. By traditional Islam we understand the historical form of Islam, which is characterized by the combination of national traditions with Muslim norms, recognition of religious pluralism, harmonious coexistence in a secular society. The leader of traditional Islam is the Spiritual Administration of Muslims of Kazakhstan.

There is no confrontation between the state and traditional Islam. The analysis shows that their relationship is based on two principles: 1 - the principle of non-interference, 2 - the principle of cooperation on topical issues. The increasing importance of the relationship between the state and religion is confirmed by the transformation in September 2016 of the Committee on Religious Affairs of the Ministry of Culture and Sports into the Ministry of Religious Affairs and Civil Society (hereinafter - MDRGO), to which the functions and powers in the field of interaction between the state and religious organizations, the civil sector and youth organizations were transferred. Already in February 2017, a bilateral agreement was signed between MDRGO and DUMK. The essence of the agreement is summarized in the words of Minister Nurlan Ermekbayev, who outlined the Ministry's focus on the organization of joint work with the Muftiate to conduct activities aimed at preventing the spread of religious extremism, implementation of additional steps for the spiritual and moral education of the younger generation and the involvement of religious associations for this purpose within the framework of measures to ensure the security of society, as stated in the Address of the Head of State to the people of Kazakhstan in 2016 [5]. The answer of the Supreme Mufti correlates with the words of the Minister: "This agreement provides an opportunity to effectively conduct awareness-raising work on the prevention of religious extremism and terrorism through the cultivation of traditional spiritual values among different social groups, including young people" [Ibid.] As we can see, the core of the agreement was the problem of preventing and countering religious extremism and terrorism. The fact that this problem should be solved "not only by the DUMK, but first of all by the government" [6, p. 71] [6, p. 71] back in 2005, Mufti Absattar-Kazhi Derbisali said. Legitimization of Islam did not guarantee its high authority among the Muslims of Kazakhstan, and the emergence and activities of new movements even undermined the existing level. DUMK itself was interested in rapprochement with the state and joint counteraction to non-traditional directions in conditions of weak level of its religious and missionary activity. Now this struggle in coalition with the state can contribute to the rehabilitation of traditional Islam, raising its status and strengthening its legitimization. However, the state, having assumed the main burden of responsibility for the fight against extremism, is unwilling to limit itself to traditional methods and means (e.g., force) and is trying to influence Muslims through the influence on the modernization of traditional Islam, based on paternalistic relations.

For normal functioning, any organization seeks to be formalized, receive funds and have a social base. Regardless of the type of state (secular or theocratic) and regardless of confession, religious organizations seek to exert political influence. The Spiritual Administration of Muslims of Kazakhstan interacts with the state, as for the implementation of its fundamental goals - existence and influence, public activities are necessary: registration of organizations in state bodies, obtaining land plots, conducting business, educational, enlightenment and missionary activities, organization of Hajj, international relations, etc. The Spiritual Administration of Muslims of

Kazakhstan interacts with the state. DUMK does everything for adoption of necessary laws and decisions. In order to achieve the adoption of any decision by state bodies, it is necessary to get approval of this or that activity from the Muslim community.

The activity on joint religion, dissemination of doctrine can be carried out in the presence of a certain influence in society. The activity of a religious organization always correlates with the interests of a particular political force, which determines the building of relationships between religion and social institutions. As a result, DUMK is provided with infrastructure - Internet sites (23 sites recommended by MDRGO), Asyl arna TV channel and the program "Zh^ma yaFbi3bi" ("Friday Sermon") on the air of "First Channel Eurasia". Accordingly, one can find here near-political information as interpreted by the clergy.

Muslim clergy has a direct influence on mass political consciousness through the content of religious sermons in the media, as well as speeches on behalf of the spiritual elite. In the minds of believers, clerics represent the main novices in religion, providing organized communication with God. Their words cannot be questioned. For many Kazakhstani people, once detached from religion, the surahs of the Koran read by imams in Arabic are perceived as sacral incantations, which strengthens the authority of imams and enhances the legitimization of the content of their sermons. This is especially true for those mullahs and imams who received their spiritual education abroad and are fluent in Arabic. The DUMK forms in its parishioners worldview, psychological, and value attitudes that determine various aspects of social activity, including political activity. All this creates conditions for the dependence of the political behavior of believers on the political positions of the DUMK.

Through organized infrastructure, the DUMK is able to draw public attention to some issues and divert it from others, as well as to interpret them to benefit itself or its allies. For example, in mosques during Friday prayers, political sermons are common before important political events. This was first openly discussed in 2011 before the referendum on the extension of President Nursultan Nazarbayev's term in office. Then representatives of the DUMK admitted that a week earlier in large Kazakhstani mosques there were sermons during Friday prayers (outside their annual plan of sermons), calling Muslims to actively participate in the referendum. As DUMK spokesman Ongar-kazhi Omirbek explained at the time, "At present, the whole nation is talking about the referendum, and we too have decided to talk about the referendum, since the Kazakh people support the President for his services" [7]. The DUMK spokesman quite confidently expresses a political position on behalf of the entire Kazakh (Muslim) people.

Despite the fact that traditional Islam is not a political structure (does not have the goal of seizing state power), it has its own political position, like any organization - public or religious. By expressing its position DUMK approves or disapproves, legitimizes or does not legitimize the actions of this or that political entity. For example, at the funeral of Heydar Dzhemal, the chairman of the Islamic Committee of Russia, a famous Russian theologian and co-chairman of the public movement "Russian Islamic Heritage" in Almaty, there were no representatives of the Spiritual Administration of Muslims of Kazakhstan [8]. We believe that the reason for this behavior was the socio-political activity of G. Dzhemal, who on the one hand sought to integrate the entire Islamic world, on the other hand - justified the activities of suicide bombers. G. Dzhemal participated in the Dissenter Marches in Russia, and in 2010 he signed the Russian opposition's appeal "Putin must go". Before the funeral, the media reported that G. Dzhemal would be buried in Kensai, where many famous Kazakhs are buried, however, for unknown reasons, the funeral was held in a small cemetery in the upper part of the city. DUMK, through such revisionism, showed its attitude not only to the personality of G. Dzhemal, but also to his religious and political views, indirectly hinting to the Kazakhstani Muslim community about their unacceptability (illegitimacy).

When considering politics as a public activity, the purpose of which is to gain, retain and use power in society, the DUMK is not only a political subject, but also a heterogeneous social structure with politicized ties. Analysis of official DUMK documents denies this, but in practice it is possible. Thus, in 2011 the Spiritual Administration of Muslims of Kazakhstan spoke out against the legislative ban on prayer rooms in state institutions of Kazakhstan, which is provided for in the seventh article of the law "On Religious Activity and Religious Associations" adopted by the Parliament of the Republic. The statement was made by the Supreme Mufti of Kazakhstan himself at the time, Sheikh Absattar Haji Derbisali. The DUMK insisted on changing the seventh article and even submitted its proposals, but the Senate rejected them. The reaction of the DUMK was a statement that the Department will continue to insist on changing this provision, explaining that, firstly, the article may cause irreparable damage to the unity and harmony of Muslims in Kazakhstan; secondly, the introduction of a ban on prayer in state bodies, educational institutions and dormitories may provoke the emergence of forces hostile to the state; thirdly, it is not quite a good solution to the problem of combating extremism and terrorism. At the same time, the DUMK has supporters in the form of public organizations. A number of NGOs demanded that the document be revised and that the head of the Agency for Religious Affairs (ADR), Kairat Lama Sharif, be dismissed. The international human rights organization Freedom House said that the new law on religion violates the right of Kazakhstanis to freedom of religion and in its statement asked the Senate to reject the bill. The OSCE Office for Democratic Institutions and Human Rights (ODIHR) also stated that the law "On Religious Activity and Religious Associations" adopted by the Parliament of Kazakhstan limits the freedom of religion in Kazakhstan and will be a step backward in the commitments of Kazakhstan and the OSCE [9]. In the current situation, the main intrigue was the discussion of the new law, and the institutionalization of religious activity in the Republic of Kazakhstan has reached a deadlock. Two conditional poles have formed in the issue of further confessional development in the country.

The confrontation did not last long. After the law was passed in October 2011, the incident was settled in favor of the state. There was no broad discussion. However, from October to the end of 2011, three terrorist attacks were committed in Kazakhstan by representatives of radical Islamist movements.

A little more than a year later, in February 2013, the head of the DUMK A. Derbisali resigned before the end of his term, explaining that he wanted to engage in scientific and educational activities. The opinion of the new Mufti E. Mayamerov on the Law "On Religious Activity and Religious Associations" is still unknown, but in general, his loyalty to the state policy is unambiguous.

In the framework of our study, the importance of this or that personality holding positions at different levels in the DUMK structure is important. The actions of clerics with power determine relations not only within the DUMK, but also in the region as a whole, since the behavior of the inhabitants of the region largely depends on the behavior of believers in it. Some social processes that originate in the mosque can continue in other social institutions, becoming politicized in the process. The structure of power in the DUMK is actually built by analogy with the state executive power: oblasts are headed by regional imams, districts - by district imams, in rural areas - by village imams, which creates conditions for building relationships between secular and spiritual authorities at different levels.

There are many subdivisions represented in the structure of DUMK: 2517 associations, 2415 mosques, 1 university, 1 institute for advanced training of imams, 9 madrasas, 2 centers for training of Quran reciters. Each subdivision has its own structure and influences public consciousness in various forms. It is necessary to take into account the fact that there are different interest groups and pressure groups within the DUMK. Many factors play a major role in the heterogeneity of the views of DUMK members regarding various issues. For example, all DUMK clergy can be conditionally divided into two large groups - those who received religious education abroad and those who received education in Kazakhstan or CIS countries.

At the present stage in Kazakhstan, the large-scale legitimization of Islam is associated with the strengthening of the religious factor, rather than the factor of religion. Despite the sharp growth of quantitative indicators (the number of believers, religious organizations, mosques, etc.), it is not religion in its essence, but the political, social projection of religion that is in demand [10, p. 59]. Religion not only creates projects of acutely relevant problems that are politicized in other social institutions, but also politicizes itself, gets involved in politics, turning into a pressure group that protects the interests of personal and allies. Politicized religion can be more easily drawn into politics and turned into an active political subject.

Experts are already sounding the alarm about the deviation of the DUMK from its true functions and its preoccupation with "earthly matters", and this is a direct path to the emergence of new risks of confrontation (including extreme forms) both within the organization and in relation to other actors. Statistics show that "quantity does not change quality". For example, in South Kazakhstan region the number of mosques is approaching one thousand. However, it was the southern regions that were hit by the epidemic of abandoned babies in 2015-2016. Similarly, in the southern and western regions, where the number of mosques is on the rise, the number of pedophile crimes has increased by 50% or more. Apparently, this sector of spirituality is not regulated by quantitative records; qualitative ones are needed. Among other things, today's children in many families are introduced to religion at an early age, which is greatly facilitated by the abundance of the mentioned objects of worship. However, this fact does not affect morality. Thus, according to surveys conducted by the United Nations Population Fund (UNFPA) in Kazakhstan, 64% of Kazakhstanis had their first sexual experience at school age. And if in 2010 the number of cases of unwanted pregnancy was 28.3 per 1,000 girls aged 15-19 years, in 2014 the figure of 34.7 in this age group was registered [11].

In our time, the negative attitude to DUMK and contradictions within DUMK are primarily related to the political component, more precisely, disagreement with the existing power of the Muslim community, or dissatisfaction in its cooperation with the secular authorities. Consequently, we can make a practical conclusion about the need to improve the legal regulation of the activities of religious associations, aimed at their depoliticization and a more or less clear definition of the boundaries of secularism. The universality of politics predetermines the existence of political behavior of public organizations. Many organizations of different levels - from international to local - are politicized, and there is nothing negative in the fact that the DUMK seeks to influence politics. On the contrary, as many experts and politicians note, the participation of official Islam in the political life of Kazakhstan can affect the quality of public policy.

Nevertheless, religion and missionary activity is the main activity of religion, and the human soul is its main object, the vertical "man-God" is the main strategic concept of religious faith. Success in these spheres is the main criterion for the effectiveness of a religious association, otherwise, its existence loses its meaning. Religious association in the case of transformation into a politicized or commercialized entity becomes illegitimate in the public consciousness, and primarily in the minds of believers, causing negative phenomena.

Thus, the Spiritual Administration of Muslims of Kazakhstan has a significant impact on political processes in Kazakhstan and acts as a political subject. Transformation of DUMK into a political subject is conditioned by a complex of internal and external factors. The activity of DUMK forms not only the worldview, but also specific socio-political attitudes and stereotypes that influence the political behavior of the Muslim community and other citizens.

Literature

1. Kulakova T.A. Involvement in publicity as an innovation of public administration in Russia // Tambov: Gramota, 2011. No. 8 (14): in 4 parts. CH. II. C. 132-136.

2. http://bibliotekar.kz/istoriki-kazahstana- partii-shura-i-islami-i-shura-i- ulema.html (accessed 27.03.2017).
3. Salafis in Kazakhstan: ban, expel or...? [Electronic resource] // URL: https://365info.kz/2016/06/salafity-v-kazahstane-zapretit- vygnat-ili/ (date of address 28.03.2017).
4. KNB counted 24 radical Salafi jamaats in Kazakhstan [Electronic resource] // URL: http://minbar.kz/article/show/id/2092.html (date of address 28.03.2017).
5. https://www.zakon.kz/4844330-mezhdu-ministerstvom-po-delam-religijj.html (accessed 08.04.2017).
6. Vilkovski D. Arab-Islamic organizations in modern Kazakhstan: external influence on Islamic revival: Monograph [Text] / D. Vilkovski. Astana - Almaty: IMEP at the Foundation of the First President, 2014. 192 c.
7. DUMK implemented the clarification about the referendum outside its annual plan [Electronic resource]//. URL: http://rus.azattyq.Org/a/dumk_ongar_khadzhy_kazakhstan_mechet_referen dum/2283603.html (accessed 28.03.2017).
8. http://rus.azattyq.org/a/28158621.html (accessed 14.04.2017)
9. http://www.nomad.su/?a=3-201110030015 (accessed 04.04.2017).
10. Burova E., Kosichenko A. Actual problems of the development of the religious situation in the Republic of Kazakhstan / Edited by Z.K. Shaukenova. - Almaty: IFPR KN MES RK, 2013. - 137 c.
11. Ibrayev A. More mosques, is there more spirituality? [Electronic resource] // URL: http://www.nomad.su/?a=3-201603100023 (date circulation 04.05.2017).

Printed by Books on Demand GmbH, Norderstedt / Germany